Hunter

Robert Hunter Fitzhugh Jr.

HUNTER

*The Yukon Gold Rush Letters
of Robert Hunter Fitzhugh, Jr.
1897–1900*

EDITED BY ANN CARMICHAEL

NEWSOUTH BOOKS
Montgomery

NewSouth Books
105 S. Court Street
Montgomery, AL 36104

PUBLISHER'S CATALOGING-IN-PUBLICATION DATA

Names: Carmichael, Ann Carlisle, editor. | Fitzhugh, Robert Hunter, author.
Description: Montgomery: NewSouth Books [2020].
Identifiers: ISBN 9781588383372 (paperback) | ISBN 9781603064095 (ebook).
Subjects: Fitzhugh, Robert Hunter. | Gold Rush—19th Century—History. |
Letters—Biography. | Explorer—Biography.

This book was originally published in 1999 in slightly different form
by Black Belt Press, with the ISBN 1-880216-44-2.

Printed in the United States of America

In memory of
James Pryor Smith
1930–1995

Contents

Preface

NEARLY FORTY YEARS ago, Nancy Smith, the choir director at my church, gave me typewritten copies of letters written by Robert Hunter Fitzhugh Jr., who had left the South in 1897 and traveled to Alaska in search of gold. Nancy had the letters because her husband, Harwell Fitzhugh Smith Sr., was Hunter Fitzhugh's nephew. Nancy and I intended to edit the letters and preserve them. Before we found time to finish the project, Nancy Smith passed away—but I never forgot the letters from "Hunter."

Some years later I decided to undertake the editing myself. I wanted to work from the original letters, rather than from the typed copies which had been transcribed by Hunter's sister, Mary Brockenbrough Fitzhugh Smith. I learned from James Pryor Smith, Nancy and Harwell's son, that the entire collection had been donated to the Elmer E. Rasmuson Library at the University of Alaska, Fairbanks.

I was able to obtain photocopies of the papers from the University. The collection consists of some twenty-seven letters, numerous newspaper clippings, and other documents such as those included in the appendix to this volume—a letter of the stock offering for the purpose of financing the Alaskan venture; a telegram from the Alaska Commercial Company notifying Colonel R. H. Fitzhugh[1] of the death of his son; a letter from Edward J. Knapp to the Fitzhugh family, and a fragment of a letter from a Mr. Drake, Hunter's partner in Alaska.

This edition retains the spellings in Fitzhugh's handwritten letters, except where spelling corrections appear within brackets. To the degree that it was

---

1   At age twenty-two, R. H. Fitzhugh Sr. was a captain of engineers on General Robert
     E. Lee's staff during the Civil War.

possible, his punctuation has been retained. One of Fitzhugh's particular idiosyncracies was the omission of the apostrophe. Also, he was sparing in his use of commas, periods, and paragraph breaks.

Notes in the margins of his letters have been added at the end of the transcribed letters. Editorial guesses for illegible words are placed within brackets or are footnoted to indicate that the information was taken from the earlier typed copies of the original letters. Indecipherable words are indicated by empty brackets.

Footnotes have been used for the identification of people or for sources of information available to the editor. An itinerary, maps, and a number of period photographs and illustrations are included to aid the reader in tracing the route of Fitzhugh's travels into the Klondike and Alaska.

It is obvious from reading the letters that some are missing, but Hunter's outstanding storytelling ability carries the reader through his tale despite some gaps. It is amazing that these letters were written at all, when one considers that they were written by hand, with only candlelight or the light of a campfire and after hours of exhausting, physical labor, many times in subzero weather!

I wish to acknowledge the kind assistance of Paul McCarthy, University Archivist and Curator of Manuscripts, University of Alaska, Fairbanks, Alaska, in providing copies of the original letters and other papers; Ralph O. Bennett of Juneau, Alaska, for providing the map used on the title page and for other research; and Dr. Richard Anderson, Professor of English, Huntingdon College, Montgomery, Alabama, for his time, his skills, and his wise counsel in his capacity as adviser for this project. Most importantly, I wish to thank my family for their enthusiastic support of this project.

Introduction

WHEN GOLD WAS discovered in Rabbit Creek, a tributary of the Klondike River, in 1896, it took a while for the news to spread because that region of the Yukon territory is so remote. But by July 1897, rumors of great riches had reached the U.S. and gold fever quickly raged. Thousands of adventurers rushed to what had been a virtually unpopulated corner of the world but which within a year boasted 25,000 or more residents.

The rumors of great nuggets of gold just "lying about" were more or less true: some $100 million of the precious metal was mined over the next ten years. But there was great hardship, too. Conditions were far more brutal than most expected; near-famine existed in the cold, cold winter of 1898. Crime and squalor were commonplace. For all those who struck it rich, many others simply struggled to survive.

One of those who neither struck it rich nor survived was a young Virginian named Robert Hunter Fitzhugh. However, like another famous name connected with the Yukon—Jack London—Fitzhugh left his descendants riches in the form of vivid writing about the gold rush experience. The letters that follow tell the final three years of Fitzhugh's life. It was a great adventure.

ROBERT Hunter Fitzhugh, son of Robert Hunter and Agnes Dade Fitzhugh, was born in Petersburg, Virginia, on December 26, 1869, in a "house on Washington Street, near the bridge."[2] He lived in Petersburg, Richmond, and other locations in Virginia. His family moved to Lexington, Kentucky, about 1886. Hunter lived in Lexington for a short time before moving to Birmingham, Alabama, to practice civil engineering and to become the assistant city engineer. He later became assistant city engineer at

---

2   Information from a copy of pages from the Fitzhugh Family Album.

Evanston, Illinois, where he got the first news of the Yukon gold rush. By September 1897, he had helped organize and was the Chief Engineer of the Arctic Mining, Trading and Transportation Company of Chicago, Illinois. He set out for and reached the Klondike after a journey which would have defeated a lesser spirit.

His letters describing his journey and the subsequent months in camp are excellent examples of American literature. Hunter Fitzhugh was an educated man with a very perceptive mind, and his letters provide a firsthand account of an important part of the history of America's last great frontier. He wrote in an intensely personal style, using vivid descriptions interspersed with typically Southern expressions which give the letters a sense of authenticity. It is amusing to note that several members of Hunter's family were writers, but he thought he couldn't write. However, he had a healthy ego, and his insistence that he couldn't write was perhaps somewhat tongue-in-cheek.

To Hunter, going to the Yukon in search of gold was a high adventure, and his quest for romantic excitement comes to life in his letters. The most outstanding feature of his writing is his unflagging sense of humor. Even under the severest hardships, he wrote with a fresh, quick wit that belied the danger and the grueling, backbreaking drudgery of life in this wild, unsettled frontier. His writing is somewhat reminiscent of that of Stephen Crane, but it is most like that of Jack London. He mentioned in one of the letters there being a copy of London's The Son of the Wolf in his camp, and he recommended that his family try to obtain a copy of it.

His sense of humor was second only to his determination to find gold, and it enabled him to laugh at himself even in the most grim situations. He wrote, nearly always, with that high humor that gives the reader a feeling of optimism and hope. Only toward the end, when others were finding gold while he was not, does he express his despair. Another crushing blow occurred when some of his "friends" jumped his claims. He had been so impressed with the generosity and kindness of nearly all of the men with whom he came in contact, and the thought that those whom he trusted deliberately cheated him out of his claims was disillusioning. In his last few letters there almost seems to be a foreboding of the tragedy that was to follow. There was some evidence of his being homesick, but even during these times his humor came through. The following is an excerpt from his December 24, 1899, letter.

> It is almost impossible to believe that this is that greatest of all nights Xmas Eve, when I used to go to bed clothes and all and lie awake 10 minutes thinking it was so many hours and then suddenly wake up realizing it was Xmas Day, out I'd tumble "all standing" and dash madly for my stocking.
>
> But after all there is not such a difference between then and now, in fact there are points of resemblance. I go to bed all standing and dont go to sleep as soon as I would like, when in the morning I eagerly look into my socks to see what the mice have brought me, and I always find split peas, dried potatoes, rice chips etc.

The name "Hunter" seems almost prophetic. The reader will learn that he dearly loved to hunt for birds and game. But, more to the point, he was hunting for gold, and he was hunting for his place in the world. For Hunter, the Alaska adventure was a time of finding his manhood, a seasoning process, a time of growth and testing of himself. It was his personal journey, and he writes about it with an understanding of the growing drama.

To best sum up his character, the reader is directed to the following excerpt from the November 12, 1900, letter to Mrs. Fitzhugh from Mr. E. J. Knapp, the lay reader at the St. Andrews Mission, Rampart, Alaska.

> I first met your son a little over a year ago, soon after I came here from New York to work as a lay missionary under Bishop Rowe, and the friendship which we then formed for each other I hoped would be one of long duration. It brought me much that cheered and encouraged me in my work, and I hope and believe that it helped to cheer him also.
>
> Your son's disposition was one of the brightest and sunniest. Even in the midst of many discouraging experiences he had a high courage that was altogether admirable. He had a keen love for all that was noble and good and true and was fearless in expressing his aversion for whatever was the reverse. He loved the beautiful in nature and had a feeling of sympathy for the young which made it easy for him to gain the friendship and devotion of children.

He was unselfish and would go out of his way to do one a kindness. He loved his family and home and would often speak of them, and, best of all, he was a Christian man and was one of the few men in camp here who attended the services of the church regularly and who, when the opportunity offered, came to the Holy Communion in obedience to our Lord's command, "Do this in remembrance of me."

HUNTER

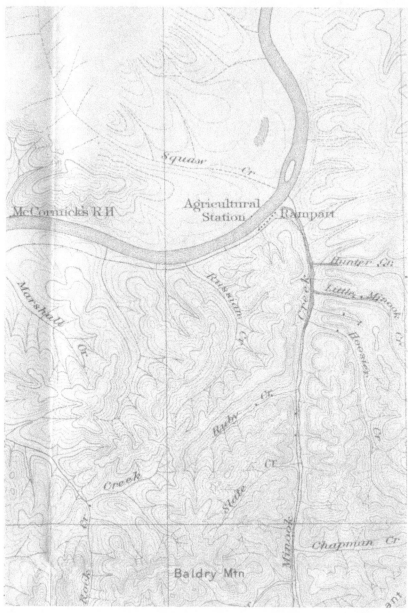

Part of a 1913 U.S. Geological Survey map showing Rampart (also mentioned as Ramparts or Rampart City), Little Minook Creek, and Hoosier Creek, all mentioned in Hunter's letters. Hunter Creek, between Rampart and Little Minook Creek, was not named for him.

Outfitting the Dream

A very fine hotel by far the finest in the city! R.H.F.

Hotel Ryan, St. Paul, Minnesota
Sept 5 1897

Dear Mother[1]

This is what you might call the first Epistle from St. Paul and it reads as follows. I have just had a most luxurious bath and shave in my room in this A 1 house and feel bully. I had prairie chicken, boiled clams and trout for my breakfast which I still feel in spite of the fact of having around my bowels of compassion[2] a buckskin money belt containing $96500 coin of the realm Im going at this thing in sort of a backwards crawfish style but have so much to write that I am all mixed up. Well after three days of buying and arranging for my departure as well as selling stock I got off on the Wisconsin Central R R last evening at 625 my fare including sleeper all the way and meals arranged for about 100 apiece was all prepaid and my baggage was attended to by the company so I was in good shape to take things easy I slept from 9 OK[3] to 7:45 this a m and feel fine. This p m at 4:30 I will take the N. Pacific for Seattle so I have plenty of time to see this burg. As is always the case I was much gratified at the solicitude expressed

---

1   Agnes Macon Dade Fitzhugh
2   This expression is taken from the New Testament, I John 3:17. Fitzhugh apparently just liked the expression because the usage here is totally out of context.
3   Fitzhugh uses this abbreviation for o'clock in several places.

by the multitude. My friends couldnt do enough for me and the way they bought stock when they heard that I was to be "old man" was wonderful. Even at the immense stores in Chi.[4] where I bought my goods the force from cash girls to floor walkers were swarming about me like flies, the pretty sales girls put on my funny looking head gear and the small boys scalped Indians with my savage looking Bowie knife while the salesmen and floor walkers shot Buffalo with my rifle and revolver. Oh we had the Dickens of a time the elevator boys, private police, regular patrolmen, [ ] "con" men doctors, lawyers, merchants, theivs [thieves,] etc all bade me good luck and god speed, if God does Bless me one hundredth the amount he has been asked to do so I'll be the whole thing up in that fearful country, it is wonderful how so many people knew I was going, you would think that in a city the size of Chi one mans affairs would not be of the slightest interest to the 1,800,000 others but I was the most prominent man in the city for awhile any how. I will have to buy my provisions in Seattle as it would cost me more than they are worth to send them out there. I may change my plans to suit the case when I reach the coast as I dont want to put $40000 with that transportation company just for one winters board if can help it.

I have letters to more people than you can shake a stick at letters from people I dont know to people I never heard of and whose only address is Alaska. A man met me on the street and gave me a letter written on a card in pencil to his uncle, I never heard of either of them before.

Now before I forget it I must talk business, I sent you yesterday a package containing my insurance policy which is paid up to next Febuary [February] after that time Crenshaw will keep it up for me, also certificates for 20 shares of AMT & T Co.[5] stock I have 30 shares but have left 10 with the company 5 to be used in keeping the power in our hands and 5 to be sold at the best figure possible the money about $7500 to be sent to you for emergencies in case you had to go the bed side of some body in great danger for instance or for any purpose which you know I would put it to besides this there is a list of my supplies and outfit which I send to save lots of writing you

---

4   Chicago

5   Arctic Mining, Trade & Transportation Company 160-162 Washington Street, Chicago

might let the family see it all around as I have such an enormous amount of writing to do and such a short time to do it in that I couldnt get around. Now within the next few weeks John and Chas [Weyward] will send you somewhere about $3500 maybe more maybe less which you are to use as follows in case it is $3500 keep $2000 for your trip to Mobile and the other $1500 to be put in Xmas presents as usual in case there is more make the division about in this proportion. I want you to have the regular amount $2500 I always give the girls if it can be managed so dont be bashful about using it all up. Ask Mr Graves to keep the papers for me in his safe. You are welcome to read whatever you come across in my papers.

If any body is hurt that I didnt write to them just say for me that I simply couldnt do it I write every minute now I got a fine telegram from "Pa" yesterday and will write to him and you too from Seattle.

In case you want to know anything further about the plans of the company write to Percy Crenshaw Pres AMT & T Co. as per letter head on circular. Send mail to him to be forwarded in case I have an address. I am traveling in fine style and have plenty of money. Tell Sallie Bryan that she is pretty if she is fickle but nevermind she will want me when I have a bushel of nuggets.

Your loving son
Hunter

Ft Wrangle [Wrangell]⁶
8 Sept 18/97

Dear Mother

Here I am in Wrangle Alaska at last we got here night before last in a
dismal rain but the newness of my surroundings kept my mind off of the
unpleasant features. I am pleased with this town although every body else is
cussing it on general principles, the town contains about 500 people 350 of
whom are Indians, it is build [built] in a crescent following the curve of the
bay. The Indians live in rather nice little frame houses—much superior to
the cabins of the negroes in the South they nearly all speak English though
the old people can hardly make themselves understood at all Chinook is
the common language on which Indians and whites meet it is very easy to

---

6   Fitzhugh used more than one incorrect spelling of Wrangell. After this correction, his
     original spelling will be used.

Fort Wrangle, Alaska

*Chief Shake's house
with totem poles
in Fort Wrangle.*

learn but it sounds like the speaker was suffering from a bad cold as the sounds all come from the throat with a sputter

The queerest thing about the whole town is the "Totem Poles" they are made of cedar trees about two ft through and 35 ft high and are carved into all sorts of the most grotesque designs one of them—the finest one here—is surmounted by the figure of a man with an intensely Hebrew nose wearing a stove pipe hat three ft high the latter painted green. Just below him is the inverted figure of a frog painted a most gorgeous green—the body of the man is black—below the frog is a bear pure white from out of the pit of his stomache a small green frog hangs half way out below the bear and frog is a terrible creature with the beak of an eagle and the body of an alligator this combination is red the bottom of the pole is decorated with a Chinese god sportily dressed in blue and white all of these are cut from the tree and are well executed. Most of the poles are uncolored and some few contain only one figure on top. Everything that breathes is represented on the outlandish contrivances.

The object of the poles is to keep up the genealogy of the family of some dead chief if the animal adopted by his tribe is a bear his totem has a bear on top if that of his wifes tribe is a frog that comes just below the small totems can be bought and I will bring one home with me. The Indians do some beautiful work in silver and have their bracelets on as pretty as any white man could do.

Mr Otterson and Koford and myself have been busy every minute—in the pouring rain—building boats for our next move up the Stickine river.[7]

---

7   The spelling is sometimes seen as Stickeen. Most maps and other publications use Stickine.

The riverboat **Aurora** *delivering construction materials to St. Michael, Alaska.*

The River Steamer may not run and if she does will charge us $5000 per ton for our outfits and $2000 per man to take us 140 miles up the River to Telegraph Creek where we strike a 75 miles portage across the country. As we will not have such prices forced out of us we just pitched in and went to making boats. We have finished one that will carry a ton and have begun another twice as large all in a day and a half for two men Koford is n g [no good] for work but a good fellow the boats when done will cost about $1000 each hr the 1/10 man[8] so we dont worry. About 75 people from the States are here making boats to go in by the Stickine trail this winter and a better lot of fellows I never saw they are all workers and are willing to give you any thing they can spare and offer to help every body that needs it we have a regular ship yard and the tools are common property no body knows his from his neighbors and they use anything they see, all of us are dressed in the typical miner style, heavy boots hobnailed, corduroy pants blue flannel shirts and sombreros also whiskers mine are just getting in good condition for the wind to toy with. The Indians tell us we will have plenty of moose and deer shooting besides the geese and ducks which are plentiful about here. My trip up on the City of Topeka was the most pleasant experience of my life and even if I should come back ragged and busted Ill be glad I came. We left Seattle Sunday at 9:30 p m and struck down the Sound to

---

8   unclear

Tacoma then turned and went north. We reached Port Townsend about 10 oclock Monday a m and lay there two or three hours, time enough for a lot of us to go fishing. I caught a flounder and several Rock [Cod] that look like Brownies by the way these little Indian boys look exactly like Brownies. After leaving Port T we sailed north again through the most beautiful scenery, the mountains rise right out of the water on both sides. The sound is from one to 20 miles wide and they are often covered with snow which gives them a look like chocolate drops with the chocolate broken off the top showing the white sugar. We reached Victoria Vancouver about noon Tuesday and stopped two hours. I went up in the Bloody Blooming British town and nearly went to sleep from the drowsiness of things in that out of date burg it is quite a city but as slow as a snail they dont open the stores until 10 oclock in the day and close them early in the p m, there is only one good thing about the place and that is the Parliament Building it is grand, built of pure white limestone and big enough for the U S instead of a miserable snow bound province. On our way up we saw several whales and multitudes of porpoise. Part of our trip was through open sea and it was pretty rough but it never made any change in my internal affairs.[9]

---

9   There was no signature. The abrupt ending suggests that some of this letter is missing.

Ft Wrangle Sept 25/97

~~Dear Mama~~

Here we are back in
Wrangle again after a few days
boating and camping trip and such
weather I hope never to see again
We left here last Tuesday noon with
three men, two boats and about 2 tons
of outfit, at first for three miles we
got along ~~finally~~ rowing one boat and
towing the other behind us, then it began
to rain - it rains all the time here - and
we were soaked. Wrangle is on an island
about four miles from the main land,
across this stretch of water we had to
row. When we were within a mile of
the main land the tide went back on
us and created a whirlpool against which
we could make no head way we sweat and
pulled until we were ready to drop, but the
land got further away in spite of all we
could do finally we struck fast on a sand

Reproduced first page of Hunter's September 25, 1897, letter.

The Journey

Ft Wrangle
Sept 25/97

Dear Maw

Here we are back in Wrangle again after a four days boating and camping trip and such another I hope never to see again.

We left here last Tuesday noon with three men, two boats and about 2 tons of outfit, at first for three miles we got along finely rowing one boat and towing the other behind us. Then it began to rain—it rains all the time here—and we were soaked. Wrangle is on an island about four miles from the main land across this stretch of water we had to row. When we were within a mile of the main land the tide went back on us and created a whirlpool against which we could make no head way we sweat and pulled until we were ready to drop, but the land got further away in spite of all we could do finally we stuck fast on a sand bar and had to stay there for several hours in the rain tired and hungry at last we got afloat again and after a terrible pull landed a long distance below where we aimed, then began the work. The current around the bluffs, all the shore is bluffs, was awful and we could make no head way against it, so I got out and took a line from the boats and pulled them for a mile against the worst rapids I ever saw. I'm used to hard work but that pull was a hundred per cent worse than any thing I ever saw. I had to climb over rocks that were slippery with sea weed and stood straight up from deep water; it would have been fearful for a man to attempt it having only himself to look after, but with that rope slippery and stiff tied to me, with three tons dragging at it the other end, you can imagine what a picnic it was, I forgot to say that before we started I lowered all that freight 20 ft down to the boats from the wharf with a new rope and it cut through the skin of my hands until they bled after that the oars were bloody where my hands touched them. All of the work was done by Otterson and myself alone as the other fellow was worse than useless never having done any work in his life and didn't seem very anxious to learn besides he coundnt swim and was scared nearly to death when we were out at sea. But to proceed with the story. We worked along over rocks and trees until dusk and when we landed in the rain at what seemed to be a nice level camp ground but we found that it was a delusion for the long grass covered about three inches of water—and the rain kept a falling; as it was impossible to find a dry place on the level we took our tent to the top of a rock near by and put it up. You can not imagine a worse place to camp than that rock it was the hardest rock I ever saw and was covered with a foot of soaking wet moss which we moved and discovered yawning caverns all through it, but we could do no better so made our beds on the rock and then started to cook supper, but to our sorrow could find not a splinter of dry wood, every thing was soggy with water and it rained all the time. We finally made a fire by splitting wood into small pieces and drying each one over a candle, made coffee ate cheese and wet crackers then "turned in," but I had to sleep between two men on a narrow blanket my head on one rock my feet on another and two feet of abyss where my seventh vertebra ought to have rested, besides this, our good for nothing Newfoundland dog squeezed between us with his wet wool in my face and snored as loud as possible all night, and the rain still rained.

Next morning we got up tired and stiff and dined sumptuously on crackers ala water then went to our boats in the rain and found them beached 20 ft from the water, left high and dry by the tide. We pitched in and unloaded them, launched them, again loaded them, and started off—all in the rain. After awhile a breeze sprung up and we hoisted sail, then for two and a half minutes we were happy except for the rain; suddenly a squall swooped down on us and carried away our rigging, then the sea began to make and in a few minutes [we] were tossing about at a terrible rate, all the time getting further from land. Only two or three times in life have I thought that I was near the evergreen shore, but when we lost control of our boats and they began smashing against each other and shipping seas every second I thought my time had come and was wondering how it would feel to be on the bottom of the sound with my mouth full of sand and fishes swimming through my anatomy toying with my vermiform appendix, but we got out of it only to get into a more dangerous predicament, for the wind drove us on the rocks of a lee shore and we nearly lost everything by the pounding of our boats against the rocks, of course all this time we were working like demons and were so tired we didnt care a cent whether we got out or not. The kid Koford, a 180 lbs six foot Englishman was nearly crazy with fright and that was cheering to Otterson and myself of course. We managed to get a line ashore and I pulled the boats up the shore a hundred yards when I ran up against a perpendicular bluff that was unclimbable so we sent the "kid" over the mountain above the bluff and Otterson and myself worked the boats along by holding to the cracks of the rock until we got to where another gang was stuck fast, afraid to let go and unable to go further; well we tryed [tried] all sorts of schemes for getting on, three hundred feet more would have brought us to the mouth of a stream and safety, but it might as well have been three hundred miles, for we had gotten to the last possible hold in the rock; at last an old Indian and his squaw came up in a canoe and we paid him a dollar to take a line ahead and hold it until the boys went around, then we were hauled out of danger,—I forgot to say that it was raining all this time. We [Well] that sort of thing kept up all that day and the next until we got nearly to the mouth of the Stickine where we struck such an awful current, the river being unusually high that we lost ground instead of going ahead, we tried for several times to stem the current and finally had to give it up so we camped in the rain and wet ground for the night. There were five parties of us and we all camped together. A worse played out set you never saw. It was hard for me and I am used to camping on any thing that will hold a tent, but the new fellows who had never slept from under a roof were absolutely miserable. My feet were dabbling in a purling brooklet all night and my 20 lbs of macanaw [mackinaw] blankets were soaked, the rain came through our badly put up tents—we could [not] get enough ground to stretch them and we were soaking wet as usual. Well to finish we all sailed back to Wrangle in four hours, what it had taken three days to go, and here we are all safe and sound, as for me my hands are raw and stiff but aside from that I am in the finest health and spirits you ever saw. My appetite is something frightful and the way I get away with broiled venison, fried flounder and clams would give you Jim jams. To sum up we worked harder for four days than many men work in a lifetime and were never dry for one second but I wouldnt have missed it for any thing and am going up that river if it takes all winter. Our plans now are to take the river steamer if possible, which is not likely, failing that we will hire Indians to take us up in canoes. If that dont work we will pull our stuff up on sleds over the ice when winter sets in, but we will go some way if all these ways fail, the other parties that came back have sold their outfits and have given up in disgust. I am enjoying everything—but the rain. I went fishing this a m and caught 15 flounders a big star fish several bull heads and horse mackerel. We eat venison here instead of beef. You ought to see me now. Im a beauty, my beard is long and flowing and I havent had a bath in two weeks It is raining now the dry spell seems to be broken. The scenery about Wrangle is beautiful everything is islands and snow capped mountains. I am in hopes of getting some mail by next steamer but may not. My hands are so stiff and sore I can not manage a pen at all. Send this letter around. I coundnt write another to save me I have fattened 6 lbs and feel splendid.

Your loving son Hunter

Telegraph Creek B C.
Oct 17/97

Dear Father[10]

This is the country of glorious health, spirit breaking weariness and boundless hospitality and I am perfectly delighted with it though to a person of Mother's disposition it would be a place of torment   there is hardly a common comfort of life to be had for love or money and this little male settlement is the only thing in shape of a town for [some] 200 miles the nearest town being Wrangle 180 miles away and it is only a frontier town of log houses 200 white people and 200 Indians. We never see a paper until it is at least a month old and I have not heard a word from home or Chicago since September 8th.

There is only one white woman in this town of 150 people and she is a Jewess who came up with her husband along with us but the men[11] are the kindest I ever saw although they all dress in buckskins and mackinaws and seldom wash.[11] What is one man's is the property of all and a perfect stranger will come over the trail and walk into the first camp he sees and take dinner without introducing himself everybody is supposed to be hungry and as soon as a man is sighted away up on the mountain trail a doz. coffee pots are set on the fire and a delegation goes out to ask him all sorts of questions that a Chicago man would resent as a most impertinent liberty. I have just cooked supper for two men who came over the trail from Glenora—12 miles South and now they are sewing buttons on with my material and one of them is putting on a dry pair of socks I loaned him. Talk about Christians but I've seen more real downright Good Samaritanism here than I ever knew existed. And then in pulling our boats up the Stickine—which is the very heaviest work in the world—it is a common sight to see a party leave their boat which has just been hauled over a terrific rapid at the cost of hours of muscle splitting labor and go back over the slippery mossy boulder and

---

10   Robert Hunter Fitzhugh, Sr.

11   These three words are illegible in the copy of the original. Mrs. Smith's transcription has been relied upon.

Approaching a tunnel (still in use today) on the White Pass and Yukon Railway.

all hands pitch in and pull some other perfectly strange party up going over the frightful work out of pure brotherly feeling. Talking about pulling boats—I suppose you read my letters to Mother about our experience out of Wrangle. Well the whole 160 miles of river is just the same only more so.

It falls at the rate of four feet to the mile, making it[12] from 7 to 10 miles per hour and in many places the mountains form perpendicular walls on either hand. The wildness of the country is entrancing, a man can climb

---

12   The copy of the original is illegible. Mrs. Smith's transcription has been relied upon

almost any mountain and feel sure that no man has ever set foot there before as there is no reason for their going there. The glaciers are perfectly grand and you can see the Glacial and Champlain period at work the tops of the glacier are covered with dust and small stones accumulated by the action of the ice undermining the cliffs on each side causing the formations above to fall, but I cant understand why the detritus and sand should always be in a line along the center while the sides are fairly clean. We saw tracks of bear, moose, caribou, and mountain sheep now and then but saw no game bigger than swans geese ducks and eagles. We were put ashore at Glenora by the steamer as she could go no further so we camped there 75 strong and stayed three days then we got an Indian to take our outfit up to Telegraph Crk for $1000 per ton we helping him. So we started off at about 8 a m three of us pulling the boat with a rope walking along the steep rocky bank sometimes the current was so strong that the boat would pull all three of us flat on the ground and drag us backwards along the shore this thing kept up—in the pouring rain until dark when we were three miles from this point then the trouble began we couldnt see our hands before us and the walking was something frightful even if a man had no load and day light in his favor but tired almost to despair soaking wet our hands cut by the small sandy rope slipping down on the rocks every few minutes, was something that a person who hasnt been to this country cannot possibly conceive of. We had had no dinner and no supper, and I verily believe I would have eaten raw dog. We met an old Indian who was loaded with dried salmon after much talk

River rapids between Lake Lindermann and Bennett.

Waiting to cross summit of Chilkoot Pass, 1898.

and begging he let us have a small partly spoiled salmon for 50 cents. This we ate raw and enjoyed more than tongue can tell finally at about 8 p m we stopped opposite Telegraph Crk and when the Indian guide told us to get in the boat to cross the river we all fell flat on the wet rocks and didnt move for some minutes. Such utter agonizing, deadly weariness I didnt believe it was possible for mortal man to endure, but we got through O K and felt fine next morning, but I didnt finish my tale of woe when we landed here we had to carry all our 2000 lbs of stuff up a steep bank 50 ft high and put it in a warehouse, then we went to the main store of the town and met Mr. Calbreath the proprietor who told us that he had not had supper and that he would cook for us too. So we sat by the stove took off our hip rubber boots dried our socks and began to feel human but awfully stupid presently, Mr. C came in with a pitcher of hot claret and sugar and we drank it all, contrary to my habit also to that of Otterson but if it had been strychnine I would have swallowed it and died in a few minutes Mr C came in and announced supper but none of us could get up the intense strain of 12 miles of boat pulling along with the wetting had "set" our joints like tripod legs get sometimes and we were helpless but finally we got things agoing and had the best supper in the world, hot coffee with cream and sugar fine moose steak stewed chicken—canned but splendid—maple syrup and beans. I— well whenever Calbreath sees me he begins to tell the crowd about my accomplishments as an eater. By this time I felt equal to 20 miles more of Stickine or anything else so we concluded to go back in the canoe with the Indian and be ready to get the rest of the stuff up the next day so at 9:30 we got in the boat and rowed back with the current reaching Glenora about 10:45 being an hour and a quarter going back where it had taken 12 to get up. Next day the Indians took up our stuff except what we could carry on our backs and we walked over the mountain trail with about 30 lbs in our packs and let me say right here that when you read about the miners going over Chilkoot Pass with 150 pounds on their backs that if it isnt a lie then there are giants in these days. The trail we followed is a good one as trails go but it "want no parlor floor" let me inform you. It follows the top of the bluff over the river all along and of course was up and down the difference in the altitude between the highest and lowest points being about 2000 ft but at least we got here and Mr. C. let us have an old cabin which we fixed

Yukoners at the summit of Chilkoot Pass (ca. 1897).

up then put up our tent along side to cook in as three more men were to share the cabin with us and there was not room for so much stuff, well in a day or two we had everything ship shape and have been living high ever since I never felt so well in my life and my appetite is a curiosity. Otterson is a good cook and between us we get up some fine meals. The clumsy fellow who started out with us and who was in mortal terror all the time is I am glad to say on the back trail we scared him out.

A few days ago Mr. Calbreath asked me if I would like to go big horn sheep hunting with him and of course I jumped at the chance so he got a young Indian to help us and taking my 7 ft round tent we started down the river in a canoe—these Alaskan Indian canoes are simply wonderful being dug out of a solid cedar log they are from 15 to 50 ft long, beam in proportion and have a three or four foot rise fore and aft they take a cedar log cut about a third of it off the top then burn and gouge it out until it is about 1-1/2 in thick they then fill it full of water and throw in red hot rocks which causes the water to boil and the wood softens they then spread out the sides to the proper shape and brace it out, finally they turn the boat over and shape up bow and stern giving the craft as beautiful lines as the most expert ship builder could make. They carry from one to 5 tons in them. Well we went down the river about three miles and landed "cacheing" the canoe then the dogs were each packed—about 40 lbs each with our cooking and sleeping outfit and we started up the steep bank. I carried my 12 lb mackinaw blanket my rifle a hunting knife and sheath axe the others about the same. We walked about three miles through the worst tangle of burnt pines and willow I ever saw and I felt sorry for the poor dogs for they would jam in between snags and fallen trunks every minute or two and would howl pitifully until they were freed. At dusk we camped and I put up the tent while the Indian fixed supper. Here a funny thing happened, the frying pan was taken from one of the dogs and put beside the fire—we all saw it, but ten minutes later when we went to use it it was gone, and to this day of grace has never been seen I think one of the dogs carried it off to some secluded spot where he could lick it in peace but the others say no.

Next day [we] scrambled through swamps and over bluffs and burnt

land until about 3 ok when we reached the outlet of a canon.[13] Here Calbreath said he would stop and set up camp while the Indian and I took a
short hunt. We were then about 1500 ft above the river and it was cold
the creek being frozen where it was still—so Johnnie and I took our rifles
and went forth walking up the canon for about two miles but as we saw
nothing, Johnnie proposed going up above timber line and looking for
sheep so up we went and wandered about in two feet of snow only to find
cold moose and bear tracks but no game so we came back to camp, and
found a roaring fire made of big pine logs 10 ft long and a bucket of tea
boiling. They drink gallons of tea up here and boil it, but the bread! Shade
of Miss Portia defend us. As the frying pan was lost Calbreath had gotten
a big boulder put it near the fire until very hot and then after greasing it
had put on the dough which he mixed by the way on a tent fly. Well that
bread was the dirtiest, rawest heaviest and best you can think of as the
dough was too soft it would do the toboggan act off that rock and down
into the ashes then we would fish it out and put it back having some of it
on the stick some on the ground, and the rest huddled in a gloomy mass
on the rock but it finally got to a point after a good mixing with dirt where
we could get a piece off without pulling a rope of dough along with it and
I never tasted nicer bread. After supper we smoked and jawed awhile and
then turned in rolling up in our blankets on a foot of pine boughs. While
we were eating supper it began to rain and snow and the mixture soaked
through all night besides the four big, wet dogs all slept with us and shook
themselves every now and then. One she dog—may her tribe decrease!
snored so loud I couldnt sleep so the Indian and I got up about midnight
made tea and smoked. The Indian told me a long story about the old wars
between his tribe and the "Taku's"[14] which was very interesting. Next day
the Indian and dogs stayed in camp while Calbreath and I went out we
had no coats on and no gloves on as the least exercise makes you red hot
here. We climbed up a mountain to its very top taking six hours to do it

13 Variant of canyon
14 A warlike Indian tribe which came to Fort Wrangell, made illegal "hootchenoo" (liquor)
    and started a gun battle with the Sticine Indians.

and the last 2000 ft was an experience it is a lot better to read about than to go through. When away above timber line in seven ft of snow the sky suddenly became dark and a heavy fog surrounded us so that we couldnt see 20 ft. Then it began to get cold and in a few minutes a most terrific gale was blowing bringing with it a cold mist it kept getting colder until I should think the temperature was about 15 degrees above 0 and the gale was so strong we had to lie down with hands and feet spread out to kept keep from being blown 8000 ft down into the canon, finally the weather grew more reasonable and we began to look for sheep but saw nothing as you know is usually the case. So we started back— the wind having sprung up again suddenly I saw a most beautiful white bird which I knew must be a Ptarmigan, fly almost from under Cs feet. Now as I was a "Chu chorco" a new comer or tenderfoot I wanted to kill the first game. So I began pulling at my rifle to get it out of its case but it was frozen so it took some time, meanwhile C who had not seen the Ptarmigan thought I was crazy and keep [kept] yelling to me to know what I saw, then he began arranging his battery for action finally I blazed away at the bird but the wind was so terrific I couldnt hold on him so missed him I fired again and hit him in the same place then C caught sight of him and began a raking fire with his new shiney improved long ranged high power etc rifle and always hit him in the place I did the bird meanwhile mincing along like a tame pigeon and was never more than 100 ft from us. Well to make a long story short I shot 11 times at that cussed fowl and C 7 times but his ammunition cost 10 cts per load, only to see our bird calmly sail away to the bottom of the canon with every feather in its place.

After scrambling through the wall of cartridge shells that lay around us we went a few hundred yards further when I saw three more Ptarmigan—C didnt see these either—so I picked out one which was sitting on the snow and aimed at his head, just for amusement of course. I didnt expect my ball to stop this side of the canon but to my surprise he flopped about like a chicken with his head cut off so I hurried to his assistance thinking that the sudden noise had rattled him so he couldnt fly I was just about to tell him wait a few minutes and C would be along with his fine new etc etc gun and that I thought it would amuse him more than my common 44 cal

Winchester of the vintage of 87, when to my consternation I found that he had no head.

I picked him up and walked back up to C with an I-always-shoot-this-way-when-I-want- to expression and showed him my bird telling him with a grand flourish of the hand that there were two more of them down below and that he might get one too. Well he started out to look for the others when his moccasins slipped out from under him and he skooted about 200 ft down the mountain right on top of the birds which flew to some place unknown. We went back to camp in a heavy snow storm and ate some more dough a la ashes rolled up in our blankets and slept with dogs once more. Next day we came back through a heavy rain the Indian killing a big blue grouse on the way, by the way we cooked the Ptarmigan for breakfast, it was a little larger than a pigeon and there were three men and four dogs to eat so we put him in about two gallons of water, with a lot of dried onion rice, dough and bacon and lived high. The Indian who never heard the word 'Ptarmigan' calling them "white chickens" was convulsed with laughter at that stew he said—"two gallon water tenos (little) rice, tenos onions and one tomahawk thats what white men eat."

All this time I had been wearing heavy hob nailed boots which were stiff and cut my ankles terribly so that walking on the mountain sides caused me great pain. The Indian had made fun of me for wearing them at first but came to the conclusion that they were not so bad when [remainder lost]

Unknown prospector panning for gold in a creek in the Yukon.

In the Yukon

Telegraph Creek B C
Oct 22/1897

Dear Evelyn[15]

I sent Mother today a black bear skin the former owner of which was killed just out of town along with her two cubs [for] their little skins. My now partner Mr. Geo Otterson once of Ga but directly from Hawaii very fine looking a good cook and married sends you these two baby skins as a present. He says you may make any old thing they are big enough to make of them or use them as foot rugs on cold mornings. I might have said that I killed the bears but as I didnt think it best to say that an Indian rejoicing in the name of Skookum Jimmie fired the fatal shot. Tell mother she can do as seemeth her best with the She Bear's hide. It is a genuine Ursa Niger[16] product and would be worth $4000 in Chicago. I dont know when she will get the pkg as I will send it down the river 160 miles by Indians then it will have to go via steamer down Puget Sound to Seattle. It would alarm you to see the prices of things here. Brooms $100 wash tubs $250 flour 20 cts per lb Bacon 50 ct chocolate drops $150 per lb etc.[17]

There isn't a woman in town barring numerous Pocahontases except a

---

15 Evelyn Lee Fitzhugh, youngest sister of Robert Hunter Fitzhugh, Jr.

16 Black bear.

17 The first paragraph of the copy of the original was illegible. Mrs. Smith's transcription has been relied upon.

Kloochum boarding a boat on the Yukon at Rampart.

Jewess we brought along with her husband—and not a man wears a coat or shaves there is not a frame house in town—all log and everything is straight up and down our cabin and tent hung 70 ft above the main town.

I went to a dance on what we call 400 Hill night before last and it was out of sight there were about 20 Indian bucks 15 Indian women or (Kloochuun) a half dozen half breeds and a dozen or so of us whites. The seats were trunks and boxes around the walls and the illumination two candles the men were all dressed in blue flannel shirts and mackinaw pants—no coats—and the ladies in the loudest rigs you ever saw with beads every where they would stick. Compared with the Thlinkit[18] Indians of Wrangle the "Stick" Indians are quite pretty one of them Kitty lives next cabin to us and is really good looking. She said to me Micah Cuttus Boston man during the dance which being interpreted means "You are a no good white man" because I couldnt dance with her. I made a mash on her by giving her a can of condensed milk that was so strong it was breaking up our kitchen furniture.

---

18   There are several spellings for this tribe in various publications. This appears to be the most accepted.

Talking of kitchens reminds me that Otterson does the cooking and I am flunky. He gets up the best sort of meals this morning we had fried salmon the lightest sort of hot cakes genuine maple syrup and fine imported coffee. We live high now and will until winter comes on in full blast. I am fattening so fast that I feel my extra weight very sensibly. I went hunting twice lately staying five days once two days the other time but only killed a few Ptarmigan and grouse. I carried a 50 lb pack on my back for 15 miles over the worst road you ever saw. Some times I had to hold on with both hands and feet and once with my mouth. Another fellow and I thought we would climb out of a canon about 2000 ft deep at a point where it seemed to be barely accessible. So we started climbing straight up the loose trap rock wall but when we had gotten about 100 ft up the whole business below us gave way and went crashing down the canon, then began the trouble. We couldnt get down as there was nothing below us and everything above us was loose and giving away. I had my 50 lb pack my rifle a big hunting knife and a sheath axe which seemed to be pulling down in spite of all I could do.

Finally my hands began to give out and I could find nothing on which to put my feet so I let go one hand and felt for a point of rock below me. I fully expected to fall to the bottom of the canon and was so exhausted I didnt care much but luckily I found a crack in which I jammed the stock of my rifle and then used it for a step this gave me a breathing spell and I managed to crawl up a few ft further to where a small birch tree grew out of a crack as soon as I got safely behind this tree my companion in misery called out For Gods sake help me the rocks are falling on me. I looked down and about 10 ft below poor Billie was hanging with one arm mashed between two big rocks and the other holding back a big chunk of trap that was slowly settling down on him. I didnt think I could do him any good but I cut the tree against which I was leaning and poked the top of it at him holding on to the stump with one hand and on to the big end of the tree with the other. Billie grabbed the top of the tree with one hand then worked his arm out of the crack and began to pull up the tree hand over hand finally getting up to me. After that we made our way to the top of the mountain where we both lay down for a long time with out saying a word. The strain on my arm was so terrific that I couldnt use it for two days afterward. That was the closest call I ever had and I dont want another. By the way a party of four men started out from Wrangel some weeks ago in a boat and after working as only Stickine "tourists" can work were upset in Porcupine Rapids and one man was drowned. Their outfit was lost. This is a country of terrors but thank heavens I and my man are safely over the bad part of it. It only remains to go to Teslin Lake 150 miles over a first class trail which we will tackle within a month or two. The only mail I have gotten since Sept 8th was two letters from Chicago written Sept 9 the mail came via Indian canoe in a soap box and it would have amused you to see the escort of 75 men who marched down to the river to receive it. I was disappointed in not getting any mail from home but expect another canoe soon. How is my Mary getting along? Give my love to all Daingerfields, and kiss M Darby for me. Write to me via Wrangel c/o [McKenna]

                                                                Hunter

Telegraph Creek B C
Nov 7 / 1897

Dear Mother

I dont think I will have time to write a long letter as the Indians are loading their canoe for Wrangel and it dont take long to load Indian canoes.

I am still charmed with this frontier life and am getting heavier every day also, my whiskers which are about twice as thick as father's and are considered very 'tamed' here.

We have a new man with us now—a Japane or Japanese or Jap whatever they are. He is a graduate of some California school of miners and is an expert assayer and chemist. He started from Japan about four months ago along with an American assayer. They headed for the Yukon River with a splendid outfit of assaying implements and a lot of fine seal skin clothes, which the "Jap" says cost him $60000 besides two years' provisions, but when about three miles from Wrangel they were struck by a squall and to save their lives had to throw nearly every thing over board, but they came on up the Stickine any how reaching here last week with only 100 lbs of provisions and the clothes they wore besides a few assaying tools and their guns. The American found that it would be impossible for them to go on, and he tried to get the Jap to go back down the river but the Jap was too game and said "me go home Japan no see gold country. Just same die" so Otterson and I proposed to him that he go with us and we would outfit him for 12 months he to give us 1/3 of whatever he found and to do whatever work we wanted him to do. So he stayed and we are charmed he is the best all around man I ever saw he is an "out of sight" cook and wash woman and is the most humble, grateful man I ever saw, he is correspondent for a Okayama Japan paper and is an educated man yet he treats us just like the old time darkies treat the white people. It is all we can do to make him eat at the same table with us and I had to tell him that I would be mad if he didn't use the blankets we gave him and he is certainly cleaner than either of us because he washes now and then. I think that with him we can find the great mother lode of which so much is said.[19] He wrote a long letter to the Japanese paper in which he said that O and I were the best white men in this country, and he tells me that if I were to go to Japan he would give me a letter that would make all the Japs bow down and take off their hats to me—how nice.

He wrote to his father last night and told him to send you something from Japan so I gave him your address which the old Jap will paste on the pkg, so look out for a pound of tea or rice.

News reaches us of a big "find" just about where we are going so we will be in it.

I am cooking in the blacksmith shop and sleeping in Johnnie Hylands nice little cabin and am as comfortable as you please. I forgot to say that with what little stuff the Jap saved and the $60000 cash he had as well as the things given him by other campers, we had plenty of stuff for him.

I could write you a mile about the Indian girls and the dances. The former are the Jolliest mortals I ever saw and are really witty, but their morals—Ye Gods! the dances are perfectly ridiculous. I can talk to the Indians perfectly in Chinook now much to the envy of the other fellows who dont catch on so easy. As to Mary B.C. she's all right So am I, but as may not see the states again for some years she may be Mrs. some body else by that time.

The Indians are singing their crazy goodby song so I must hustle. I got letters from you and MBC last week the first for months.[20]

Lovingly Hunter

---

19 The last half of this sentence was illegible. The transcription of Mrs. Smith has been relied upon.

20 This portion was written along the side.

Hotel Northern, 117 First Av & South Victoria, B.C.[21]
December, 1897

Dear Mother,[22]

I am waiting for the S.S. Topeka to go up to Wrangel when I will return
to the frozen North.

I staked out a quartz claim for myself and five other fellows then came
down to Victoria to have it recorded. I find it is 'dilate cultus'—not satisfactory. So I will go back and get some more claims. I was out on the trail
nearly all the time for the past two months and I wish I could write you all
of my strange and ridiculous experiences but it would take acres of paper,
oceans of ink and horse powers of work to do it up in style. I stayed out for
twelve nights with the mercury ranging between 0 and 35 degrees below,
sometimes with only the blue above me and never under a roof our best
house being a 10 x 14 canvas thrown over some poles stuck slanting into
the snow. I was with one white man and two Indians and enjoyed it nearly
all. Coming back to Telegraph Creek I got into an Indian village late one
night and was taken in by an old Siwash who gave me a big dried salmon
some tea and bread which I devoured in a lump   the tea was given me by
an old squaw who stirred it with her never washed finger but it was good I
slept that night in the same room with five Kloochuun (women) three men
and 9 dogs but after I dropped on my blankets all was a blank until next
am when I found that the dogs had done those things which they ought
not to do all over things but that was all right

Well it was while on this trip that I laboriously staked out our claims
and the day after I got back to Telegraph Otterson, Fred [Borln] an Indian
boy (Dick) and I started off down the Stickine with three sleds each pulled
by two dogs. I was in the lead to pilot the gang and break trail and I held
that position for the 150 miles down the river to me belongs the honor of

---

21   Supplied by his sister, Mary Brockenbrough Fitzhugh Smith
22   The first two pages of this letter are missing, but the letter appeared in the Lexington,
     Kentucky paper. From the beginning down to "get some more claims" in the sec-
     ond paragraph was copied from the newspaper clipping, according to Mrs. Smith's
     transcription.

breaking the trail down the river this year. It is a job that old timers look upon with dread and they nearly jumped on my neck and wept when we started. They said that Blizzards or thin ice or Hudson Bay winds or snow slides or some other old thing was bound to do us up but we didnt do up worth a cent. It was my first experience on snow shoes and I had been dreading my first attempt to walk on them, but I put them on and just lit right out from the jump and left the whole brigade Siwash, dogs and all far in the rear. We were 15 days making the trip down which was not bad for the time of year though we expect to make it up in ten days or less as the ice will be perfect then

I broke through the ice more than a dozen times sometimes in ten feet of water but every time I got out easily in spite of snow shoes and other impedimenta. Some times the snow was 7 ft deep and the travelling was fearful but at other times we found only a few feet of snow and a fairly good crust to walk on. We camped in about six ft of snow every night. We would scrape out the snow for a space about 10 ft by 15 sloping it from its natural surface at the back of our "fly" to the ground in front, in this

Riverboat on Thirty Mile River

Prospectors starting for the Yukon from Juneau (ca. 1896) carrying their snowshoes.

low place we would build a fire of big logs and the heat would be reflected from the sloping roof of our fly down on our bed of fir boughs covered with canvas. All four of us Siwash and all slept together spoon fashion and when any one of us wanted to turn over he would sing out all turn! and over we would go. It is a queer country you dress to go to bed and undress on getting up. I put on my mackinaw coat a fur cap and an extra pair of moccasins at night but during the day wore no coat and only one pair moccasins and a sombrero. I was in a drenching perspiration all day and had to stop and fan every few minutes. None of us washed for 17 days or took off our clothes for 20 days but you get used to that. Water is scarce and snow is not good to wash with so we gave it up. My hands are filthy yet. We met some poor fellows going up who were rank green horns and they gazed in admiration at us old hands. We gave them all pointers in a fatherly way levied an assessment of tobacco and baking powder on them and passed gloriously down the ice the envy of the new comers. Whew! I have so much to say but you cannot hear it now. Well we got to the mouth of the Stickine and found 7 miles of open sea between us and Wrangel with no boat to take us over so Otterson and I left the other two in camp on the "point" and taking one blanket and two days bacon and bread we started out over the mountains for the point opposite Wrangle Island. This sounds easy but never in your wildest dreams could you begin to appreciate what it means but we got out OK, after walking two hours making a mile and a half I found that the tide was unusually low and that we could walk on a peninsula separated from the shore by a narrow strip of water we waded this and started off down the sand when to my Crusoe like joy I saw foot prints in the sand (quotations are in order) prints [near ours] of goodyear rubber boots and new ones at that, so off we went at a trot as the tide was about on the turn and to be caught out then meant death or a ducking. To be short with this tale we found two "misable" fellows camped on a steep place by the sea having been fooled by the Indians into stopping there. They told us that a wood cutter just below had a boat and might help us so we hustled on about a half mile further to the end of the sand spit and lifted up our voices in lamentation to the unseen (I smelled frying bacon though) cutters. Bimeby as the Indians say they answered and finally rescued us it was then pouring rain but those two fellows proposed out of pure kindness to go against the tide back to the other fellows and get them that

Mail leaving Rampart by dog sled.

Dogs towing a boat at Nome.

dark windy, rainy night. So we took possession of their camped [camp],
ate their muck a muck and dried our foot wear, etc. Along about 1 OK a
m they came back with dogs, sleds, men and all. The rain was then coming
down in a solid chunk but we decided to go to Wrangel that same night as
I was figuring on getting home for Xmas and didnt want to run the risk of
missing the first steamer. Off we started down the most dangerous coast on
that string of bad [stronghes] and sounds that reaches from here to Dyea.
It was just at the point where we came near losing our outfit last Sept., and
if we hadnt put in to a little bay we would have had a bad time again, but
our pilot knowing that a storm was coming up landed us at the very same
camp ground of which I wrote last Sept. You know the wet place. Well we
had to stay two days and nearly two nights on that point of land in an old
leaking salmon house with two inches of water on the floor. We had to burn
every thing in the house salmon spears and all. I think that we were visited
by the worst gale of the season and it was out of the question trying to face
it in a small boat, we could see the steamers coming and going only four
miles off but they might as well have been 400. None of us slept a wink
for three days and we were in water up to our ankles all the time but it was
really enjoyable. I reached Victoria after a most delightful trip of 700 miles
on the S S Topeka than which a more pleasantly appointed vessel doesnt
float. Tell everybody to buy their outfits at Louch, Augustine & Co. of this
city, to stop at the Hotel Northern, and to go up on the Topeka and they

will get rich especially if they tell the proprietors and officers that they know me I get no rake off for this puff.

I reached Victoria which goes to bed with the chickens and wakes up at noon, early Sunday am and went up town to the New England Hotel. I was dressed in the beautiful costume of Ye miners, long bushy whiskers dirty hands and wet moccasins and was a fright but the populace didnt seem to be afraid for it came down on me like the wolf on the fold it asked me all sorts and conditions of questions and went forth and told it, they wouldnt let me eat nor read the paper nor smoke they cleaned my so called clothes with admiring eyes, and the next day it came out in the paper. I came down from Victoria on the S S Kingston and was prevented here for a while but am now allowed to go free as I have gotten into white folks clothes and shaved off my beard I have fattened 18 lbs in spite of my tribulations and every body says that I am looking positively portly

Xmas day I spent on the Topeka crossing Queen Charlotte Sound[23] had been five minutes faster I would at this moment have been with you all at Lex[24] but the said boat was just late enough to cause me to miss the east bound train which made me lay over 24 hours, which gave me time to attend to some business, which brought about a change of program all around and now I am waiting for the S S Topeka to go up to Wrangel where I will return to the frozen north.

I brought down some fine furs and left them at a furrier's to be mounted and sent home. I will send you tomorrow some little curios on my way down. If you write at once and address Wrangel, I may get it before I get out of civilization.[25]

Hunter Fitzhugh

---

23 Half page of letter missing
24 Lexington, Kentucky
25 This last paragraph is from a newspaper clipping according to Mrs. Smith's transcription.

Hotel Northern
117 First Aven. South
Seattle, Wash.
Jan 7 1898

Two men are waiting for me to finish this letter so they can cross question me.

Dear Mother,

I am still in Seattle as you see but will leave in a few days for the "North Countrie". I sent you yesterday or day before I forget which a pkg of pictures which Otterson and I took with a small camera. Some of them are very good but as usual the best ones were blanks. I had two large photos of the other fellows and myself taken just as we got into Wrangel with our Arctic rig and beards on but they were perfectly blank. We will take a bigger camera up this time and hope to get some good views. I write this letter more to give you some of the details of our trip down the Stickine than anything else as my last letter was too voluminous to admit of more than an outline. You will see among the pictures I sent you several taken of the two wolves, these are real Arctic wolves caught near Pt Barrow on the Arctic Ocean and brought down by a whaler. Johnnie Highland bought them and raised them for work dogs but they have been so petted and spoiled that they remind you of babies than anything else. They will howl most dismally if left alone for any length of time, and if permitted to do so will spent [spend] all of their spare time sitting as close to you as possible. The greatest pleasure in life to them is to shake hands and if you pay no attention to them they will paw you all over to attract your attention this often results in their getting one foot in your coat pocket which is very exasperating especially if you dont know it and attempt to get up off the ground. Another thing they are fond of doing is to sit on your snow shoes as they are drier than the snow, and many a time I have started off after fixing their harness or putting their feet over the traces only to go head foremost into 6 ft of snow owing to a sixty pound dog's being perched on the heel of each of my shoes. They cannot bark at all but howl like the common wild wolf. One sings baritone and the other a beautiful clear falsetto which is very nice during the day

Mail arriving in Nome.

but they always have two concerts at night, one just as we are getting to sleep, the other about day break which causes us and the other common dogs to do many things that I cannot write. All dogs in that country have to be tied with chains as they will cut a rope in a few minutes. The wolves are the most omnivorous animals I ever saw. They are particularly fond of sole leather but any sort of dressed hides delight their souls. They ate every vestige of "filling" (moose hide strings) out of my snow shoes they did likewise to one other snow shoe belonging to our Indian. They devoured a pair of moccasins and one of Otterson's beautiful Caribou gloves which he was bringing home as a curiosity, but worst of all they ate my heavy sole leather rifle case leaving only enough to cover the barrel and lock   t h e buckles and rivets were never seen afterward and the   Indian claims that the dogs ate them too. Quien sabe!

Our other dogs were just common black dogs rather small and hairy—large dogs do not pay—and it is surprising to see the way the little fellows pull a sled through deep snow and slush ice. Sometimes when the sleds are "stuck" the he dogs try to catch hold of the ice with their mouths so as to pull better. They seem to enjoy the terribly hard work they have to do and when we pack up in the morning they raise a fearful racket whining and barking in their eagerness to be off one dog (my private property) even goes so far as to poke his head through the collar of his harness before his time comes to be hitched.

The strain on a mans nerves in that country is something awful and the temptation to swear long and loud is sometimes irresistable, but at night all is peace and harmony. There is magic in a camp fire and a pipe. I had to walk ahead of the train and sound the ice so of course if any body broke through into the water I was the man. Many a time have I broken through and as I felt myself going would call to the others not to follow my trail too close but the dogs would take an insane desire to follow me and me alone, and all the yelling, swearing and beating that the boys could do wouldnt stop them until they came to the very edge of the broken ice when they would make a sudden turn and dump the sled over almost in the water. Such tricks as this almost caused our hair to turn gray but at night the dogs would sit in a solemn meek circle around the fire and blink so trustfully at us that we would feel sorry for our misdeeds and straight way go forth the next day and repeat the performance. We fed the dogs only once a day, about 8 p m giving each about a pound of rice (weighed dry) and a quarter of a pound of lard. We boiled this in the same buckets we afterward cooked our beans in and as we trusted to the dogs to lick the rice out clean we frequently found a ring of well licked burnt rice around the bottom of the bucket when the beans were gone. The sun rose about 9 a m and set about 3:30 PM so we only had five hours daylight in which to travel hence we ate only two meals per day one about 8 a.m., the other about 5 p m but ye Gods how we would eat our regular rations consisted of Baking powder bread cooked in a frying pan coffee and fried bacon for breakfast and the same thing for supper except we had tea instead of coffee, every body gradually gets in the tea habit up there. The Indians have a bucket of tea on the fire all day and all night, and the white men drink gallons of it every day.

We ran out of tobacco, baking powder and coffee about two thirds of the way down the river and strange to say we met two men who had more outfit than they could handle so they gave us tea, coffee, sugar, butter, 60 pounds of rice and best of all plenty of tobacco for which they would not take a cent. Oh yes they gave us 12 pounds of prunes and apricots and we nearly made ourselves sick eating them raw and stewed. Every gang of men we met insisted on our staying with them and we had to almost fight to keep from eating when we didnt have time. One set of fellows whom we

Crossing a crude bridge in the Yukon (ca. 1897).

had known in Wrangel—the men in the boat building picture—told us to stop at their cabin about three miles below and help ourselves to whatever we wanted, so as we got there about 3 OK, we concluded to camp there all night. The cabin was very small and full of grub and tools but was warm and comfortable. Otterson— than whom a better grub skirmisher doesnt live—rustled up the most wonderful dish you ever heard of but it was fine. He hung a big two gallon bucket over the fire and dumped in the following, seven cans of clams, two cans of tomatoes, 1/2 lb rice, four onions, 1/2 lb bacon and 1/2 bottle of curry powder besides a lot of dumplings. Well it was simply immense. We ate until our buttons wouldnt stay on and our abdominal regions felt like drums, but the next day heavens! We could hardly get one foot by the other and I got stuck in a snow drift and begged to be allowed to stay there until the river melted in the spring but the others made me go on in spite of my abdomen. I am particularly fond of canned clams but somehow I dont have that wild craving for them that I used to have.

The greatest trouble I had in coming down was in trying to keep cool. The violent exercise and heating food combined to keep me in a most un-pleasantly perspiratory condition and the dew of honest toil dripped off of me until my clothes were wet. I wore no coat during the day and no gloves but we all dressed to go to bed, putting on an extra pair of moccasins a fur cap and a coat which we took off in the morning. I am besieged by dozens of people who call at the hotel to talk to me about the trail it seems funny to me to be an old hand giving advice and information where a few months ago I was a greenhorn and had to ask others. Men come to me with letters of introduction and others come because they met somebody who knew that I had been through and they persecute me on all sides. On all such subjects as snow shoes, moccasins, camp fires, Kloochuun I am standard authority.

Mr. Bayton a fellow tourist up the Stickine gave me a letter to his sister Mrs. Baker who is housekeeper at the hotel, and he did me a good turn as well as himself for Mrs. Baker and her daughter—a very young married woman—treat me like I was their own personal private guest and I spend all my time in their big warm parlor. I have had a pretty bad attack of grip for the last few days but I am over it now. Dr. Coleman's awful calomel and ipecac did the business but the ordeal was frightful. I didnt go to bed in

Dinner time in a Yukon cabin. Note the canned onions and reused crates for Jersey Cream and clams.

fact was not in my room during the day so you know I am not alarmingly ill now. If I was feeling very badly I would hardly write such a letter as this has grown to be. I don't know what has gotten into the people in the States they are all going crazy about Alaska and it is going to result in more misery and tragedy than gold. That there is gold up there, there is no doubt, but 9 out of 10 of the people who go in will spend about $100000 in getting a few hundred in gold and the vast majority will get nothing. Yet hundreds of thousands go in without knowing the first thing about roughing it and will fall by the wayside. I am glad that I will be ahead of the great rush. I am afraid of it. Steamer passage has to be engaged weeks before hand and every boat is loaded to the gunnels.

Write as usual to Telegraph via Wrangel.

Love, H

Telegraph Creek, B.C.
Feb 24 1898

Dear Father

After a long and tempestuous voyage of 31 days on the ice I am safe again in Telegraph much to my great satisfaction. Altogether I have spent 48 days of this winter in an open tent fly on the ice and I am not itching for any more. This thing of sitting by a roaring camp fire with a big tent in the background is all very well in a picture but I'll no more of it for the fire always refuses to roar when it is most needed and the smoke nearly blinds a fellow. Some times we had to burn cottonwood and the smoke is something awful. I thought my eyes were ruined but they are OK now. We had about 1200 lbs to take up the river and it was the worst deal I ever struck as there were only two dog teams and they could not manage more than 400 lbs each. We had to pull the other stuff ourselves and nobody who hasn't tried it can conceive what that means. The first 40 miles up is through the bad weather belt where it snows and blows almost continuously and as the snow is from four to nine feet deep and no trail, we floundered along at an average rate of 2 1/2 miles per day. Some days the wind was so terrific that we had to stay in camp all day and have our eyes put out by the smoke. Our equipment consisted of four sleds, four dogs, four men, 1 frying pan, four buckets and one 10 x 12 canvas tarpaulin besides other little stuff. We figured on making the trip in 15 days but were that long going 40 miles. When our grub ran out we lived on rice alone for a day but next day fell in with some fellows who were hauling their stuff up to Telegraph. They were glad let us take a lot of their stuff up so we loaded on a lot of beans, flour and prunes and started off again but the loads did nothing but turn over in the deep snow about twice a minute and monkeying around a dog sled in seven feet of snow with snow shoes on trying to "right" a 400 lb load is one of the great trials of life so after about half a month of toiling terribly we "cached" about a third of our load and came on another 50 miles at about seven miles per day, another fellow and myself pulling 300 lbs ahead of the dogs. As this was too slow and the dogs began to play out we cached 150 lbs at the big canon fifty miles below here. After that we averaged 10 miles a day reaching here at noon yesterday amid great rejoicing.

People congratulated us and wanted to 'treat' and asked what about Cuba, and whether we had Hawaii yet, had Corbett succeeded in making FitzSimmons fight and all sorts and conditions of questions. Some we answered evasively some we lied about and others we told the truth about, it all squares up in the end. Now comes the sad part of the story we found that all our claims had been jumped by men we considered our particular friends. It seems that as soon as we were out of sight, Frank Calbreath, Jim Hayden and an old cuss named Martin whom I was particular thick with, all went out and restaked our claims and had them recorded at Dease Lake knowing that we could not get to Victoria before they had us headed off. The people here are ready at a moment's notice to have a necktie party and if it was not for the fact that most of the gang are out on the trail I think there would be trouble, but I am tickled to think the claims were failures in the light of what has happened. Our outfit will be hauled by Mr. Highland 40 miles out next week and then we will have to haul it on land sleds over to the lake work, work, work! everything is work here. I will separate from Otterson after we get as far as the lake as we dont get along really smoothly still there is no quarrel only he wants to be the "whole thing" and tries to keep me in the background as you see by the Stickine paper which was sent home. I have not had my clothes off for 31 days and have washed only a few times. The temperature today is — 32degrees but is fine. My hands are stiff and I am tired, so goodby. I will write again by next post. I am in glorious health but dirty. Write as usual to Wrangel at T.C.

Hunter

This is a jerky badly written letter but I am somewhat worried.

Indian [ ]
Mch 20th 1898

Dear Mamma: I have absolutely nothing to say. Because I am getting more sleep, I am feeling better bodily. Your postal card and a letter from Nannie rec'd today. I will leave here as soon as it can be done but cannot tell [last half-sentence is missing][26]

12 miles from Lake Teslin
Apr 28/98

Dear People

I am safe and sound fat and dirty but still decidedly in the ring. Otterson and I are safe now but havent been so very long as the river over which the last fifty miles of trails runs is breaking up fast. I didnt know that I would have a chance to send a letter in for a good while so decided not to write until I was finally in camp at the lake but as I said before we are OK now so dont worry.

The work and worry we have been through is enough to kill a mule but I seem to get fat and grow a beard on the strength of it. Mrs. Craker and Strukly will take this letter to Seattle and Mrs. Otterson will send it on. I write in camp in a great hurry. So dont criticize this effort too harshly.

Write c/o Capt. McDonald, Lake Teslin via Wrangle on T.C. Will write at length.

Lovingly Hunter

---

26 Marginal notes.

Lake Teslin, B C
May 5 1898[27]

Dear Father

This is going to be a long story, a long trail and I dont think my hand more used of late to pull a sled than to write will stand it all at one jog as we say on the trail. So I may go at this a little at a time until the whole is accomplished.

We got here May 1st after having been 57 days on the trail and the last day was the worst by long odds so far as manual labor is concerned as we had to pull 1,100 lbs over a perfectly bare trail for 6 miles. Not only this but thousands of fallen trees were lying across it all the way and torrents of water flowed along it a great part of the way, it took us 11 hours to make the 6 miles but we finally got in safe and sound but almost dead from the straining and pulling.

But to begin at the beginning I have kept 'tab' on the distances a day at a time and make it 197 miles from Telegraph Crk to Lake Teslin. Others make it 185 but I think I am nearer right than they.

I wrote last from Kakitza (excepting a pencil note a week ago) so I will start from that point30at K we counted up our outfit and found that we had 1800 lbs of stuff 1400 of grub and 400 lbs of ictas, as the Indians call general belongings. And there were only Otterson, the dog, and myself to haul all of that weight up hill and down for what we thought was 100 miles. As the trail from K is very good at the start I took 400 lbs on my sled Otterson 250 on his and the dog hauled 300 helped by O. That day we made 12 miles across two miles of pretty good portage and 10 miles of ice on the Chesley River. Of course we had to pull the empty sleds back making 24 miles in all. Next day we took our camp outfit down to the foot of the mountain over which the trail passes from the Chesley to the Doodanto River. This is 15 miles from K so we were three miles below our cache but we made a night trip up that distance and brought it down to camp. Next

---

27   The copy of the original was illegible, and reliance has been placed on Mrs. Smith's transcription.

day Otterson took the grip and I had to do the whole job myself. A job it
was too. I walked up the mountain and found that it was a little over three
miles from foot to summit and the first and steepest mile was a side hill
trail with no snow. The last two miles was pretty well snowed but was pitchey
ie full of short ups and downs that almost break a mans back. I had been
told that few men pulled 150 lbs at a load up that mountain so I started
off with that amount but the next load I took was 175 which was my regular
jog after that for which feat I was much praised by the pilgrims and one
fellow who had a horse pulled 600 for me just because I was getting along
so fast (a good chance to moralize but I wont do it now). I made three trips
a day and it didn't hurt me a bit but the way I did eat! Ye Gods! Finally we
got to the top with all our stuff and then began down hill work. We crossed
many lakes from 100 yds to 2 miles long and followed the little streams for
miles sometimes cutting off bends shooting straight over the bight of one
bend to the outside of another. These "cut offs" are called portages but I
dont think it the right word, but whatever they should be called they are
man killers for they are always bare of snow and nothing but swamp the
very hardest sort of country through which to pull a sled. We followed the
Doododanto[28] for about 20 miles in this way my load being between 450
and 560 lbs when the trail suddenly took a shoot for the dry land and for
7 miles now known as the long portage we pulled and jerked and swore and
sweat over that 1800 lbs until sometimes I thought I would go actually
crazy with weariness and agravation. You see we were too late in the season
and the Spring being warmer than usual the trail was perfectly bare in spots
from a few feet to several miles in length. Nothing that a man could write
or say could give you the faintest idea of the awful work that we had to do
on that long long trail. I can hardly believe it all now myself it seems impossible. But I must keep up the thread of my tale, or Ill be lost. Well it only
took us two days after all to make the 7 miles and then we struck Long Lake
(about three miles long). Over this I ran with nearly 600 lbs. Then we followed Mosquito Creek for 10 miles crossing more of those miserable portages.
That night we had no ridge pole for our tent and no fire wood except Swamp

---

28   Fitzhugh's misspelling

Cranberry stems about as big as your thumb. It was dark when we camped and we had made about 12 miles that day, so it was very dreary and sickening at first but we got up a meal of moose tenderloin broiled, the finest tea in the world and two dozen baking powder biscuits and life was once more endurable. Next day we took 1200 lbs down over the most perfect trail I ever saw at first but when we reached the 10 mile point the ice suddenly gave way and down I went into icy water about two feet deep then in swashed my sled, flour, sugar, and all but we got it all out safely and went a short distance further when all three sleds went in but Ill cut that short. From that point 12 miles further we waded all day long down Lost Creek. All of us had rubber boots, but I never could wear the instruments of torture so went at it in my regular moccasin foot wear, two pairs of moose moccasins and three prs sox. Of course I was soaking wet but my feet were perfectly warm. The strain on our minds and bodies during the five days it took to get through that water was maddening our lives and provisions were both in the greatest danger and the work was fearful for we had to put one sled on top of the other in order to keep our stuff dry. Well the creek was full of slush ice which would accumulate ahead of the sleds until it suddenly stopped them damming up the water until it would run over our grub. Then Otterson and I would get hold of the sleds and tug and strain until it seemed as if our backs would break but that miserable slush would hold her tight as if she was screwed to the bottom. The shovels were then used and a chute made ahead for a few feet through which we would pull the sleds. For three nights in succession as well as every day we worked at this delightful employment but at last we came out of it as usual in the best of health and without having lost a thing. Our outfit of grub is all sewed up in two water proof paraffin sacks and they did their work nobly for we haven't lost a pound by water. After our five days of wading we found that we were at the top of a falls over which we had to lower the entire outfit 40 feet O at the top and I below where the icy spray soaked me again. After the falls we followed the Niline River for 4 miles and then we took up a very steep little creek for two miles. It was a hands and knees performance from beginning to end and it would thaw out enough in the p m to get us all wet as usual. Leaving this creek we had about three miles of back breaking portage then a lake then a bad portage. This alternate lake and portage business kept up pretty regularly for about 16 miles when we struck Big Lake the first of the Yukon water shed. This lake is four miles long and empties into a small creek which discharges into the Nilzituck river which drops over a falls into Lake Teslin. So you see we were safe when we reached the lake. For even if the trail thawed out on us we could build our boat and drift right on around to New York City. But we pushed on hauling 1100 one day, 500 the next—having eaten about 150 lbs of grub by this time and thrown away a lot of boxes and wrappings. After the big lake we crossed another two mile portage and followed a small creek for 10 miles. The trail then follows the Metzachooah River 30 miles to Lake Teslin but it came near costing us our lives as you shall hear. All went well until we reached a short portage about 18 miles from here when the ice began to get very treacherous. I was in the lead pulling about 400. Next came the dog with 400 of flour and bacon. Last, Otterson came with 250 of baggage. The trail lead over a steep snow bank beyond which the river was open except for a narrow ledge of ice. I managed to swing my sled down and around to the left on this ledge in safety and stopped as quickly as possible in order to slow the dog down over the pitch knowing that if he came on over the drop the sled would shoot straight into the river but I was too late. Before I could get out of my harness dog, sled and all had plunged across the narrow space and disappeared in the swift water. So in I went too not to be gallant or to save the dog but to save our 400 lbs of provisions which are scarce in this country even now. I got a hold of the sled and managed to push it over to the other side when the dog held it by getting his fore feet in a crack but to my sorrow I found I couldn't touch bottom and the ice had such a pitch to it I couldn't get a grip on it. Besides, I was getting chilled to be bone. But something always happens at these times, you know. I looked for it and saw an old willow tree about 100 feet below me which touched the water. So I turned and made for that finally pulling myself out wet and cold but safe. O and I then went back and pulled the dog and sled out.

Coming back Otterson was some miles ahead riding the dog sled so I was alone pulling my empty sled when I had nearly reached the spot where I went in in the A M. I found that the hot sun had thawed the ice much further down and it was still more dangerous. I managed though to get to within about 200 ft of the jumping off place, when all at once the ice gave way and down I went again, this time with my pulling gear on and rotten ice all around. I tried to get free of the sled but only got mixed worse so caught hold of the edge of the ice and pushed the sled crossways in front of me, hoping by increasing the bearing to be able to crawl up on the sled. But every time I got my knee on it the whole thing would break down again. At last I thought I was done for and the first thought that flashed through my mind was why was I allowed to do all this awfully hard work up and down the Stickine and across 20 lakes only to be drowned in this miserable little stream. Then lots of other things came to my mind and I was having a nice time in general when it occurred to me to use the sled as a ladder. I had gotten out of harness then so I held on to the ice with one hand and pushed the sled down until it touched bottom then I climbed up until the ice broke always facing the shore. I kept this up until I could see the bottom and then I walked out but I was nearly gone. To make it worse I saw a hole a little further on where a man had evidently broken through and beyond it was the tracks of a sled and dog but no man tracks. Hence I argued that Otterson had gone in and stayed in but the dog had gone to camp. You can imagine what a pleasant four mile walk I had soaking wet chilled almost to congestion tired and hungry and the prospect of finding a wet dog hitched to a wet sled the only occupants of our camp but when I was within half a mile of camp I smelled the always welcome odor of frying bacon and I forgot all of my troubles. I let out a yell and Otterson answered. A few minutes later he met me in his under clothes all wet and blue looking but grining like a possum because he said he "sized it up" that I would think he was gone and my yell amused him. That was the closest call I have had on the trail but I have had plenty that were close enough. The day after this we pulled our last load over 10 miles of soft black ice making a new trail through the woods around this bad place. Next night a merciful providence sent us a pretty good freeze and we took our entire outfit to the last portage over ice as hard and smooth as glass. This left us 10 miles of portage between us and the lake and 10 miles of double distilled copper lined agravation (sic) and enormous toil it was. Just think of pulling 400 pounds from Lexington to

The Soapy Smith Gang of Skagway, Alaska. (Soapy Smith was a saloon owner, see photo with letter of August 1, 1900.)

Castleton up a hill steeper than the South Broadway hill. Think of that hill being crossed in every direction by thousands of burnt logs and the space between the logs soft and boggy with from a few inches to a foot or more of ice water standing on it. Then add a mile of winding, pitching, snowless down hill trail crossed here and there with torrents of water, and you have the tail of the Teslin Trail.

We reached here May day and an ideal one it was too warm and bright. We made the acquaintance of too [two] pligrims from Spokane on our first trip down the Stickine— they were then just coming up—their names are Shoemaker and Coolin, and nicer fellows never hit the trail.

Just here Otterson warned me to come and 'chew' before the moose got cold and you bet I didn't need a second invitation. We had moose steak broiled with onions, stewed peaches, fine sour dough bread, the best tea on the trail and Sago pudding with real raisins but it is not always thus by any means.

But to continue we toiled and hauled along with these two men—may their tribe increase!—for about 100 miles but finally they got ahead of us reaching here a few days before us. So when we got in all tired and dirty they got us up the finest dinner I ever ate, and next day Mr. Shoemaker went back and helped us bring our cache down. We are camped along side of them now and I hope we will go on down together.

Teslin Lake is about 140 miles long I think and is about 1 half mile wide at this its extreme Southern end. There are about 200 people camped on both sides and the Teslin Yukon Trading Company has just built a small saw mill across the 'chuck'. They will in fact have begun to build a steam boat to run down to Dawson. The pilgrims as we call the army of sweating, swearing, bacon eating prospectors 'one of whom I am which' are a study or are studies which ever is right. Some in rags some in tags and all in big beards and splendid health the trail is full of them and volumns [volumes] could be written of their queer ways of doing and thinking most of them went sailing by us taking their entire outfits at one jog making from 10 to 20 miles per day but there will be a sad day of reckoning ahead of them for they are all short of grub and none can be bought. Every thing is $100 pr pound salt flour bacon fruit, pitch every thing is held at the one price one dollar but that will not buy it. Thank heavens we have a big lot of stuff if it did almost break our backs to drag it here. Since last September I have walked over 1400 miles, I have pulled an average load of 350 lbs 500 miles and I think that at least 50 miles of that has been over bare swampy ground, but my health is something monumental and I am as strong as a bull, and my whiskers shades of Herr Mast defend us but they are beauties.

Swans, geese and ducks are very plentiful and I have grown tired of eating duck. My rifle is a bacon saver and each successful shot saves nearly a dollar.

Tomorrow we will go to whip sawing out the lumber for our boat this will take a day or two then we will build our vessel and wait for the final break up of the lake which will come soon.

To sum up my opinion is that this trail as terrific as it is is by far better than the Chillkoot for no body has lost his outfit and no lives lost excepting two men who were drowned on the Stickine and two who were murdered on that river, but it is a thing of the past now and is I suppose perfectly bare all the way back to Telegraph Creek. I hear that hundreds are stuck all along but they started too late. This is strictly a winter trail and only pack horses can get over it in Summer.

Mosquitos are beginning to get in the hills now and I shudder to think of what is to come. The days are very long now from about 2:30 to nearly 9 pm I wouldnt go through my past two months experience for four thousand dollars and I would not have missed it for twice that. It is no country for sick men, cowards and women and don't let any body tell you that women enjoy it. They dont and it is very trying on the men who have them in tow. You remember the story of the Confederate Soldier who saw a rabbit running to the rear during a hot engagement and who yelled at it, "go it Mollie Cotton tail if I didn't have any more reputation than you have I'd run too?" Well that is just what kept us all going on the fear of being cowards. Ive told that story often along this trail and it always meets with a hilarious applause.

It is hard for me to realize that tomorrow I dont have to pull, pull, pull at a heavy sled through brush and timber up hill and down but I am thankful to say 'Je suis j'y reste'. The balance of my journey is through peaceful waters. Selah.

I have written nothing private on the foregoing pages thinking that maybe you might want to give it to the paper. I know how they grab at Alaska things.[29] I have not heard a word from home since the middle of March and may not hear again for two months.

This letter will be taken back to Telegraph by a man who is to walk in with a pack on his back. Ive done some of that and dont hanker after nearly 200 miles of it.

Otterson sends love and says he is coming to see you'uns when he gets is [his] bag full of nuggets he also asks that a copy of the paper containing this letter be sent to his wife at Seattle, but dont have it published for my sake. I never did crave to be a newspaper contributor or notoriety[30] and I cant write much anyhow my hand is so stiff from the toil of the trail.

I left Chicago Sept 4th to go to Lake Teslin and I am here and have been much praised for the amount of work I have done. There isnt a better known man in this country than I and many fellows have promised to put me on to the first "thing" they strike. How many times while I was pulling my life out nearly wading in icy water I have thought of our parlor at home and of the guitar and the old patched up big chair upstairs and all

---

29   Part of this letter was printed in one of the Lexington Newspapers.
30   Unclear.

the little details of home. One night several of us were camped together in a dark solemn looking canon and our talk drifted to home—it seldom did. One fellow said he would sing us a song to lighten us up. Well he struck up "Rock Me to Sleep, Mother." He sang it in the most impressive way I ever heard a human sing and before he was done out of seven men five were crying. I have read of such things but I never saw it before. A man is so utterly, absolutely prostrated with weariness on the trail that his mind is almost effected [affected] by it and then the displays of temper are something terrible. My temper was never very sweet but now it is fiendish. I have had to use every bit of self-possession I could raise time and again to keep me from killing the poor dog when he had pitched head over heels down a hill with the sled. Oh it is no use to write about these things. A mile of paper and an ocean of ink would only weaken it. Im through with [ ] safe, and in splendid shape so let it drop.

Write to me at [ ], c/o Capt McDonald, Lake Teslin. Love to all. Plenty of gold now.

Lovingly,
Hunter

Lake Teslin, B.C.[31]
May 8, 1898
to W. Percy Crenshaw, Pres.Arctic Mining Trading
& Transportation Co. 160-162 Washington Street, Chicago, Ill.

Dear Sir:

I have nothing of importance to report, beyond the fact that I am at last safely located at Lake Teslin, having reached here May first. My experiences on the trail would, if written in detail, fill many more pages than I have time write, as the Indian who takes this to Telegraph Creek leaves within a few hours. Hence I give you only the merest outline of my trials and work hauling my stuff from Telegraph Creek to this point. I have kept an accurate diary of each day's work, keeping account as near as possible of the distance traveled. Making due allowance for inaccuracies, etc., I estimate the distance from Telegraph Creek to this point as a hundred and ninety-seven miles, although the majority of the "Pilgrims," as we call the Argonauts who are in search of the "Golden Fleece" up here, put it at about 180 and the government at 123 miles. Mr. Otterson and I with our dog "C.B.," hauled 1800 pounds of packages and provisions the above distance in fifty days, taking it in two "jogs," that is we would haul 1100 pounds twelve miles one day, "cache" it and walk with empty sleds back to camp, next day, moving camp up to, or a little beyond, our cache. In doing this, of course, we traveled about 600 miles, besides 400 miles which we had previously traveled on the Stickine River. For 400 miles of this distance, I personally pulled an average load of about 400 pounds. Sometimes my load reached the 600 pound mark, but as a general thing I took 450 pounds, rarely less. The trail for the most part was over swampy land, along small streams and across twenty lakes. There were three very bad climbs on the trail where it was all a man could do to pull 150 pounds. I made quite a reputation as a draft animal by regularly hauling 175 pounds up one climb of three miles, making three trips per day. The gradient of this part of the trail was about ten feet per hundred, or five-hundred feet rise to each mile of horizontal

---

31   No copy of original letter. This is from a newspaper article based on the letter.

distance. The first mile of this was absolutely bare, as it lay on the sunny side of the mountain, and the snow had entirely melted. In fact, I think I have pulled my load fully fifty miles on bare ground during the trip. The labor that a man performs in hauling his outfit in to this lake is something beyond the conception of any one who has not been here and seen with his own eyes the long procession of straining, pulling, and jerking men toiling along up hill and down through icy water up to their waists, with from 300 to 600 pounds dragging behind them.

I would not go through it again for $5,000, but that amount would not tempt me to turn back, having once set my face towards "the long end of the trail." I was twice so nearly drowned that I had almost given up hope and I broke through the ice probably fifty times. Our dog pulling 400 pounds broke through the ice, and I thinking of the calamity the loss of so much food would be to us, jumped in after him, and the whole outfit including myself came within an inch of going down under the ice for good and all. But luckily I happened to get hold of an overhanging willow tree and got safely ashore helping the dog out. At one place the trail for ten miles was along a small creek which was covered about two feet deep with a rushing, roaring torrent of muddy water as cold as ice. It was very dangerous as we could not see where we were going and the ice beneath was broken in many places, yet for five days and three nights we hauled our heavy loads through this and never lost a pound. We had to work many nights as we were afraid at times to leave our "cache" far behind fearing a flood or a thaw. So after a hard day's work, we would walk back several miles after dark to our "cache" and haul it to camp, getting in at midnight. Yet, with it all, I cannot report any ill effects from my hard winter's work, for I weigh now 160 pounds, while I weighed only 136 pounds the day I left Chicago. My health is perfect, my appetite beastly, I can eat almost twice government rations, and I can do the work of two ordinary city men. I am now engaged in whip-sawing the lumber for my boat, in which to drift down the "Diggins," and will be ready to start in a week, if the ice in the lakes is out in time. There are about 300 "Pilgrims" camped here and the Teslin Trading Co. is running a small saw-mill, the first one ever seen by the Indians in this locality so it is not so lonesome.

Provisions are both very scarce and very high, everything selling at one dollar a pound. Salt, flour, bacon, and sugar are all in demand at this figure. I have enough to run me until October, after that I don't know what I shall do. But I hope to get another year's supply some way. I have been as economical as possible with my provisions all along, hence have the biggest supply of any one man in this camp. But I fear those who are short will compel us who are not to sell a part of our outfit; however, that is not likely as pack trains and boats will be in with supplies by the last of July, we hope.

Everybody is hopeful here. The country has the look of gold, and the "colors" are found almost anywhere.

I hope to report something more to the point next time. I cannot see how I can do anything much this year, however, and think I will have to stay up here at least another year in order to have time to prospect and to work my claim, should I get one. Money is not as plentiful with me as I could wish, but I will rustle along some way with what I have.

I have heard no news later than the loss of our battleship Maine. The United States and Spain may at this moment be fighting, but we poor fellows are beyond the sound of the guns. We will probably get a mail at fifty-cents a letter in a week or so, as we were promised by the Telegraph Creek merchants that they would send the Indians in as soon as the Spring thaw was over. It is almost over now.

I saw plenty of moose and caribou signs along the trail but only two of the latter animals as they were frightened away by the bell of our dog sled and the smell of camp fires. I have lived high on the finest meat in the world for comparatively little money, as I bought a quarter of moose (about 70 lbs.) for $6.00 and it took two of us nearly two weeks to eat it. The Indians kill great numbers of moose, but they want "white man's prices" here and ask $1.00 per lb. for meat, so I don't buy any more. The lakes are full of duck, brant, geese and swans. I have killed a good many ducks which saves many a dollar's worth of bacon. There are hundreds of "Pilgrims" strung out along the trail between here and Telegraph Creek who were caught by the thaw, and they cannot possibly go until next winter as only by the most persistent work and by tempting providence that we got in. And as it was we had to pull our sleds on bare ground and fallen timber for the last ten miles of the trail. I can solemnly say, "thank God, I am here safe and sound." The rest of the trip is smooth sailing, I have reason to believe.

Write to me care of Captain C.E. McDonald, Teslin Lake B.C. via Ft. Wrangle, Alaska. I will let you hear from me as soon as possible after I reach the Hootalingua river.

Yours sincerely,
R. Hunter Fitzhugh

Queen's birthday celebration in Dawson, Canada, 1901.

Camp Victoria
May 24/ 1898

Dear Mother

This is the birthday of Queen "Vic" hence the name of this camp. This letter should be called "The Cruise of the Evelyn Lee" for that is the name of our good ship in which we sailed down the lake. We whip sawed the lumber and built her ourselves so we feel very proud of her. She is 21 ft long 4'-2" beam and is 20 inches deep carrying easily one ton of cargo. We carry one 8 by 12 sprit sail and four oars. I told Otterson to name her "The Lissie" after his wife but he said I must name her after Evelyn[32] to whom he sent the baby bear skins so we broke a can of condensed milk over her (but saved the milk) and launched her.

We left Teslin City at 9 a m day before yesterday and made splendid time running before a fair wind this far—12 miles—but could get no farther as the ice blocked the way. We may have to stay here several days if the weather doesnt change, but it is probable that we may be able to sail on tomorrow.

Our camp is on a beautiful gravelly beach and the lake stretches out for five miles straight in front of us.

Before I forget it, I met a Mr. Fripp, correspondent for the London Graphic who came over our trail—Wrangle, T. C., and Lake Teslin—direct from London to write up and illustrate the trip for the London paper. His work is fine and "shows up" things just as they are so if you can, get the daily and weekly Graphic from about June 1st until the series runs out.

Seven other fellows sailed down from Teslin City and camped with us so we have a nice little city here. A gang of us went across the lake yesterday and prospected finding colors in almost every pan but no pay dirt yet. Still it shows that we are within the golden circle. I have seen several men who came in via Dease Lake. They report good prospects within 50 miles of us and they have all cached near the ground and only came in to get more grub.

The lake is full of water fowl and we live high and have lots of fun too.

---

32   Evelyn Lee Fitzhugh, Hunter Fitzhugh's youngest sister.

Mining with "long Toms" (sluice boxes) on Nome Beach, 1908.

Yesterday the whole gang of us were lying on the gravel in the sun, telling lies and relaxing as only sled pullers can relax when somebody yelled—Beaver. The meeting rose up as one man and rushed off after guns. I got back a little ahead of the others and jumped into a boat but the beaver had disappeared so I started to land again but just then he came up about a hundred yards from me. I blazed away with my rifle and missed him several yards. Then he came up again, and again, and I gave him a shotted salute missing by a hair, this kept up some time until the beaver turned back toward the shore where he was met by a volley from eight magazine rifles, but none of them hit him. At last he made a dive and came up fully 300 yards out, when old man St Clair sent a 30-40 cal ball through his head. Thats all except that his skin is hanging over my head tightly stretched in a hoop and a large part of his carcass is deep down in my "tum tum." We eat beavers up here and they are good. Selah!

A man killed a 1600 lb moose with a pistol yesterday. They are very plentiful about here. Salmon trout pickerel and pike are getting tiresome, but flour and other muck a muck is steady at $100 per pound and no body will sell for that as a rule.

Mosquitos here are something awful and as large as swans. The further we go the larger they grow.

I am expecting the pack train in to Teslin City soon and will get lots of letters when it comes. It costs $1 apiece to send letters out and probably that much to get them.

I have many things to write but I cannot write them now. Every body who has known me for any length of time remarks on my wonderful improvement since I got off the trail and I was particularly fat and healthy then. I must weigh between 160 and 165 pounds now.

We are in a new country for Indians now. My old friends the Tahltans[33] are far behind and the Takus hold the fort here but I can talk Chinook fluently now so it doesn't make any difference what tribe I run into.

I will likely be able to write every week or two from now on address to me at Lake Teslin. Tell Father to write to Ottawa Canada and ask for a copy of Ogilvie's report on the Yukon Country.

Lovingly Hunter

---

33   This is the same tribe also known as the Stick Indians. The name is occasionally spelled Toltons, but Tahltans appears to be preferred.

Rampart City
October 5, 1898

Dear Father:

The moon is shining bright and clear over the mountains across the river the air is cold and full of glistening particles of ice. A Siwash dog is doing the wolf howl and some fellow is playing The Blue Bells of Scotland on a violin and every thing is peaceful. Alaska whatever else may be said of it is the land of beautiful nights. It is a joy to be alive now. The rainy season died a natural death last week. A two days terrific snow storm wound up the program and then came a stretch of the most beautiful weather, freezing up the boggy trails and making travel a joy. Ralph and Joe two of my partners went out to the gulch to start their own winters work and I went with them. It is 9 miles out to the gulch and when we went the trail was a bottomless swamp covered with this everlasting arctic moss. I could write a book about the aforesaid moss but I dont want to immortalize the beastly growth.

Between the three of us we carried 230 pounds of baggage picks, shovels, cross cut saws, provisions and bedding. My pack weighed 93 pounds, 50 pounds is a big load for even a good trail so you can imagine how I lightly tripped over swamp and fallen logs loaded with 93 lbs. I had to walk two frosty foot-logs across a deep rushing steam with that49 cumbersome load on my back. It took us six hours to make the nine miles and when we got there my back was almost skinless but I came back next day.

Yesterday I took another pack of 64 pounds, part of it being a six foot whip saw, and two buckets of apple butter. The latter bumped about on my back so that I couldn't tell which way to balance. The result was that I fell off the foot log when nearly across, landing forked-end down in three feet of ice water but that didn't hurt me a bit. I got used to it last winter. This morning I came back making the trip light on a frozen trail in two hours.

Minook, the old Indian prospector (rara avis) from whom the district is named put me on to a new creek about 25 miles from here straight over the mountains. He told me he had gotten 15 cts. to the pan before he hit bed rock which is splendid prospects for any country. These $500.00 per pan stories are Jonah and the Whale propositions, either 50 miracles or fabrications. Minooks word is as good as gold in this country so tomorrow Doc Hudgins and Man Peterson and I are going to make a combination hunting and prospecting trip to this creek and will likely acquire another claim apiece. I now own interests in six claims and am very likely to make a good stake before I go back to Civilization. A greenhorn who was nosing about Little Manook gulch not long ago picked up a $65.00 nugget.

A fine grown moose weighs dressed about 800 pounds and caribou 300 to 500 pounds and we can sell every ounce at 50 cents per pound so you see it would pay to kill a few. Some Texas friend of mine went out about 30 miles from here and killed a big bear. One shot did the business and the distance carefully stepped was 160 yds. The ball had gone clear through the shoulders making a hole as big as a hen egg. The rifle was one of the new kind known as the 30-30, that is the calibre is 30/100 of an inch—about the size of a bad pencil—and the charge consists of 30 grains of smokeless powder. I have seen one of these guns shoot through a green spruce tree 16 inches in diameter—they will shoot through the thickest part—and no telling how far it went after it came out. Their penetration is 38 in. in white pine, their killing range 8000 yds. with a very flat trajectory. They are wonderful guns and only cost $17.00. They are absolutely smokeless and make very little noise. I could write a volumn [volume] about guns and hunting but am getting tired of the usual occupation of writing. I have had no mail since the lot I mentioned about a month ago. They were written in May and June. I fear that it will be many a month now before I hear as the river is very low and will soon freeze up. I was most particluar to write in the early part of June from Dawson telling you all to address me here but some how I have gotten no mail. Now and then a few letters come up and the other fellows draw a letter or two but I get nothing. I am almost ashamed to ask now.

I have seen a number of papers lately and am thoroughly posted on war news from the Maine to the peace. It was a huge picnic and we did ourselves proud, but I don't think it wise to acquire any possessions farther away than Cuba. I hope we will sell the Phillipines.

We will get a two weekly mail this winter.

Lovingly, Hunter

Rampart City
October 28, 1898

Dear Ma:

The regular monthly dog mail leaves early tomorrow on its 1500 mile run via Ft. Yokun, Circle City, 40 miles, 70 miles, Eagle City, Dawson City and thence over the trail to Juneau and the P.O. cabin bears this notice, "Get your letters written for the outside mail leaves in am. PO closes at 12 o'clock." So I have a lot of letters to write I'll not make this one very long.

Winter has been on us for the past month and the Yukon is frozen over right here but has open holes farther up we hear. I keep a regular accurate record of the weather as there are plenty of thermometers here. The coldest so far is 6 degrees below. Right now it is 2 degrees below but within a month it will probably get down to 40 degrees or 50 degrees below and during January and February to 70 degrees but I dont fear the cold as I am fixed for it and the thought that there will be no mosquitos adds to the comfort of winter here.52 The sun rises at about 8 am and sets about 4 pm now. Next month it will rise at 11:50 and set at 1:30. I cannot understand why it is perpetual day for some days during the summer but never perpetual night in the winter.

I wish you could see the Indians now and some white people. They are covered head and foot[34] in furs, wearing parkies [parkas] of reindeer, mink, and hair. A parkie is a big long shirt of fur with a hood pointed at the top like monks. On the feet fur mucklucks are worn. These are big boots, big enough to accomodate four pairs of heavy socks. The uppers are of fur, "the fur side outside," and the bottoms are heelless and made of walrus hide. The little Indian children playing look like little bears. I am going to buy an Indian parkie to take home when I leave here, if Evelyn will promise to wear it down town.

My oldest partner Doc Hudgins and myself took a trip a week or two ago up Big Manook Creek and it would have astonished you to have seen our equipment. It consisted of two blankets, one small canvas, 1 pound

---

34   Parts of these sentences are missing from the copy of th eoriginal.

of bacon, 1 pound of coffee, 1/2 pound sugar, three loaves [missing], no coffee pot, or any cooking utensils, yet we lived high for an even week on this, walking over snowy mountains and frozen streams probably 200 miles in all. We killed grouse and squirrels and caught all the mountain trout we could eat besides we fed the dog on trout and grayling that would have made your mouth water. We saw plenty of signs of moose, caribou, bear and wolf but we got no big game. I fired at very long range at a splendid enormous black wolf but held too low and lost him. He had come within 50 yds of our camp.

We cooked our squirrels on forked sticks before a big camp fire and I found a lard can top on our way up, of this I made a frying pan on which I fried the trout. I also found a 1 lb corned beef tin in which I made coffee so we had a nice time although our bedding was far too light. We would spread the canvas out on the spruce boughs then the two blankets. The Doc and I would then lie down near the end of the blankets and would pull the other ends over us. It was cool for me though as we were away up in the air some thousand feet higher than here and much colder.

My eyelashes and hair would have frost on them in the am.

Claim no. 9—a pup thereof
Little Manook Creek
Rampart Mining District, Alaska,
Latitude 65 degrees, 30' No Longitude, 1500 degrees 45'W

Dear Brokie,[35]

I owe so many folks so many letters that "Gawd" knows I dont know who to write first. You people on the outside having writing desks, comfortable chairs and plenty of light, also nimble fingers from not having to earn your beans by the sweat of your hands, may think that we poor unfortunates in these sequestered everlasting ice clad mountains are somewhat remiss in our correspondence but could you look in on me at this moment you would feel that only the greatest amount of loyalty to friends and family could induce you to write under similar circumstances.

I am sitting in my flannel shirt sleeves—havent been otherwise a dozen times within the year—at our made-into-the-house dining table before a little bit of a window made of celluloid instead of glass. The stove is red hot and so am I. I am cook this   week and am at present cooking peas, evaporated potatoes, evaporated eggs, tomatoes, and corn starch pudding for which latter I have a wide reputation. The floor of this cabin is built of poles and my chair is a block of wood sawed from a spruce tree and when I get off of it it falls over. My partner Joe Bush is cussing mosquitos out of doors and also washing his unmentionables in a five gallon evaporated potato can—the national wash tub of Alaska. I washed my shirt and my other socks yester e'en so dont have to repeat the performance for at least two months. The sun never sets now and all night is just the same as all day only the mosquitos are more so if anything. The sun rises in the north and sets there also. "From the rising of the sun to the going down of the same" has no significance in this queer country.

(Page Lost)

—his own house and lot, had thousands of acres of the best fuel at this

---

35   Mary Brockenbrough Fitzhugh Smith, sister just older than Robert Hunter Fitzhugh, Jr.

Mary Brockenbrough Fitzhugh (Mrs. Harwell Ransom Smith, 1867–1942) in 1894, near the time of her marriage.

disposal and can always stock up his larder in the summer for the coming winter by a little hustling. I can take my rifle and in a few hours kill ducks, geese, grouse and squirrels enough for a week.

To be sure I long for home and civilization with a longing "that is me doom" at times but on the other hand if I was in the States I would be under the eye and hand of a boss or out of a job, either of which—[36]

I may get next to a claim this year that will net me $125,000.00 as the claim No.8 of this creek for Gov. McGan, who knows. Our reading matter consists of old magazines some of them as old as 1872. I have often wondered where all the old reading matter goes and maybe this is the answer. Maybe all the lost pines of the world find a last resting place up here too. Likewise the fourth dimension[37] and the silver question are settled in this region. Who knows.

The Yukon broke up May 22nd. and is now full of steam boats but in a few months it will again lie cold and still and another long dark winter will be upon us.

I wish I knew your son and heir Harwell, Jr. Nannie's Chu was a great tilacum[38] of mine, and I have always hoped to do the rich old Uncle act for those two boys some day. And I may yet. This is the country of paupers one day and millionaires the next.

Tell Harwell Sr. that I should think he could find time to write to me, not that I ever would answer but that dont count. Write and tell me all about my Birmingham friends. If you ever see or write to Della Dryer ask her to write me a full report of persons and things to date. She's a good girl and will do it I know. I am a bull knecked, horny hand, whiskered back-woodsman now and weigh 165 pounds.

Yours, Hunter

---

36   to
37   Copy of original is illegible.
38   Tillicum means "friend" in the Chinook Indian dialect.

Rampart City Alaska
May 18, 1899
Lat 60 degrees 30'
Long 150 degrees

Dear Father:

The hand that for two years has wielded the axe, pick and shovel takes not kindly to the pen, hence this shakey looking combination of streaks and scratches.

I have been waiting since last October for the ink to thaw and now that I can plunge my pen into the bottle without knocking fire out of the fluid I will give you a history of my doing largely intermixed with fiction and fancies.

To begin with, the River or as our local paper hath it our "Statuesque Galatea: the for many months corpse of the Mighty Yukon which has been lying in state within a marble sarcophagus is on the eve of its annual res-surection in fact "it stirs, it moves, it seems to feel the thrill of life along its keel." Rivers dont have keels but it would spoil the effect to leave out the rhyme and at any moment it is likely to begin its 2800 mile march to the sea, with its burden of dead dogs which died of eating dried salmon whose bones punctured their tum tums. Soon an innumberable caravan of assorted effects from Ft. Hamlin, Ft. Yukon, Circle City, 70 mile, Eagle City, 40 mile, Dawson City and way stations will move on to the pale realms of shade to mix forever with the elements and make the Post Quarternary coal measures at the mouth of the river.

I grow poetical when I think of the tribute this servant of the seas will pay to its Lord within the next few weeks. There will be a more unique display than that recorded by the poet, on the "Isle of Long Ago." There may be no "Broken vows and lutes without strings: and bits of songs which nobody sings," but there will be, as I said before, dead dogs of all nations and tongues on this terrestial ball, there will be tin cans in all sizes—to suit all purses—from those small in stature and large in price sealed and said to contain Extract of Beef—said beef used to wear iron shoes and pulled a street car in Chicago—to the monsters built like a sky scraper which once held the fossilized remains of some prehistoric beast whose invulnerable hide was cut into small pieces bleached and labeled Evaporated potatoes—many miles of good concrete trail have been made of this indestructible material—besides cans there will be a department of labor saving devices "Gotten up exclusively for our Yukon trade." With these wonders of science three able bodied men can by strick [strict] attention to business and great diligence accomplish the work of one puny man on the "outside." These have been solemnly and resignedly laid away on the bier of the Yukon to be borne back to Seattle and other seaport towns whence they came by men who came in here to do penance for crimes committed "outside" by devoting their lives to hard labor and whose consciences will no[t] permit them revel in the luxury of labor saving machines. Then comes lines of fearfully and wonderfully made clothing gotton up by some one born and raised [in] Australia who has read somebodies [somebody's] "Life in the Frozen North."

The procession will wind up with an imposing display of steamboats of various sizes which Mississippi River captains carefully ran aground on low sand bars vainly imagining that the ice would, like the waters of the Red Sea, divide and pass each side having a nice quiet pool in which the boats could dally and sport like a wild duck in some secluded pond secure for the future because it has not been molested in the past. Yea like all things material all these will, impelled by an irresistable force glide onward to the sea of oblivion and the peace that knows them now will know them no more forever, Selah!

May 24th.

On the 22nd at 5:15 pm the Yukon broke up and is now almost clear of ice. A few hours after the breaking of the ice the river rose 10 feet. It came up so fast that it was all we could do to haul our boats out of the way.

The "Chetco" an ocean going vessel which has been lying in our wharf since last summer has been the source of all sorts of bets and prophesies. It was generally considered a doomed vessel but some men held that she could be saved. Now she is in a worse fix—it seems to me—than she was during the break up, for she has been pushed 75 ft from the water by the ice which piles up along here about 20 feet deep, and is resting on and surrounded by cakes of ice 7 feet thick; and when the river rises to its regular flood depth she will go out imbedded in thousands of tons of ice. Nobody went to bed that night but all had camp fires along the beach and watched the great procession moving at a rate of about 5 miles per hour toward the sea.

But I havent time to spout about the ice as I am pretty busy nowadays. An old sea captain and I are busy putting in a garden and propose to make part of a grubstake from it. This is one of the most fertile countries on earth, but the shortness of the season admits of only a few vegetables being raised. I am going to put in turnips, radishes, onions, cauliflower, cabbage, lettuce, spinach and beets things of that kind grow splendidly here, 10 lb turnips are not uncommon in Alaska. By the way robins are out in force now and are just the same sassy critters they are outside. There are about a dozen kinds of song birds up here and the woods sound like Alabama.

I was appointed by the miners meeting to make a survey for a trail from here to Eureka Creek—the new diggins—supposed to be about 45 miles from town but I found it to be only 26.9 miles and made a big map of the entire route showing all the tributary creeks etc. It is the only authentic, accurate map on the Yukon River so far as I have ever heard. I was paid $15 per day for my services, but I dont do any more engineering for less than $2000. I have had the only two public jobs ever done in this district and will most likely get the balance if any. I had nothing but a 4" standard compass and a 3/ 8" rope to chain with but got through in good order although we had to wear snow shoes through dense thickets of alder and spruce for about 30 miles. We slept out on the ground three nights without tent or stove but after my experience on the Stickine that was tame.

The snow left the ground about a week ago and mosquitos are pretty bad already in fact I went hunting two weeks ago in snow three feet deep and was considerably bothered by the mosquitos.

Several men lost their lives last winter by carelessness. One party of three went from here to the Kaynkuk River last January taking only two weeks of grub. They never showed up again and about a month ago some men making a short cut across the mountain from the K. River ran up on the remains of two men which were nearly eaten by wolves. They investigated further and found a tent five miles away. In it was the dead body of a man lying by the stove he had a spoon in his hand and had evidently dropped dead from starvation while in the act of stirring something which was cook

long letters, I havent the time or material for others in the family. They are all mighty good about writing to me and let the good work go on.

have severe paralysis

Your off son
Hunter

Rampart City
July 2, 1899

Dear Nannie,[39]

I came in from a 10 days tramp out in the mountains day before yesterday and to my joy found that a mail had come in during my absence. I drew four letters from the lottery from you, Evelyn, Mother and Father. You have no idea what a relief it is to get a lot of mail and recognize the writing of Father and Mother as well as the balance. So, many men get news of the deaths of members of their families, and let me tell you before I forget it that while I dont get near all the letters you all write to me still enough reach me to keep me posted and I dont hold it agin ye when I dont get mail. I know it is the fault of the mail service so don't worry. I do my best and you do your best and that is all there is to do, between bad management, high water, low water, blizzards, and breaking up ice the mail proposition is a tough one.

A friend of mine and myself took a blanket each also our very small rifles and very little grub and started out two weeks ago to look at new country about thirty miles from here. We killed about 50 squirrels and caught over a hundred beautiful mountain trout and grayling—"Here and there a lusty trout and here and there a grayling"—runs through my mind constantly while I am wading about in these beautiful clear icy cold mountain streams "yanking" fish out. Plenty of bear and mooses hovered about our camp. We lived in a moss shack made by leaning small poles against a ridge pole which we tied up between two trees. We made a room about 10' by 12' and covered it about a foot thick with moss and you cant imagine a prettier camp with a roaring stream just in front, our camp fire popping away and the little moss thatched house beneath the black spruces. And we always had a string of squirrels, grouse and trout handing up in full view.

I staked another claim while out and will prospect it pretty soon. I have not much faith in it or anything else but it is a good rule to tackle any thing can possibly pan out in this country. You can't conceive of the cool complacent way in which a man will except [accept] a proposition up here that

---

39   Annie Mayo ("Nannie") Fitzhugh, Hunter's sister.

will likely throw the whole gear of his life out of action or make him independent for life. Once or twice I have thought I saw a good sized fortune almost in my grasp only to see it disappear suddenly like a Mollie Cotton tail through the briar patch. Yet I have never been either elated or despondent. I know positively that a man can entirely control his sensations, and this thing of saying that one must groan and grieve when beset by the "vicissitudes and mutations of this transitory existence" is all a matter of training—self repression or otherwise. This doesn't

Annie Mayo ("Nannie") Fitzhugh, one week before before her 19th birthday.

apply I think to death. Nothing can be done in that case except grin and bear it. I know from one or two experiences I have had within the last two years that dying is very easy after the first thought of it is past. I wrote Mother a very long account of my drowing experience while coming over the trail last year but she seems never to have gotten the letter.

A friend of mine found a 9 oz (about $185.00) nugget on a forlorn hope claim not long ago and since then has taken out 72 oz's in coarse dust which gives us a good deal more hope for the camp.

The "midnight sun" is blooming nicely.

You said you were asked about the laws in mining camps and about the way of getting the gold. I have just written a most elaborate treatise on the subject, so the next time your strong minded 19th century up to date fin de siecle lady friends who will understand all this about as well as I understand Delsarte Matrons, basques and Watteaus and cloth cut bias ask you about it you can give them a beautifully jumbled account of shoveling the tailings into the dam and hoisting the sluices out of the pay streak.

This is Sunday and I am pretty nigh dead with writing and I am going to quit pretty soon. I will certainly stay in another year. It is hard beyond anything you can believe but then I know that if I were to go home busted or almost so that after the first few days or weeks of thankful feelings and cleanings up, there will come that problem—"What next?" Where will I get a job etc. I have cut loose and found a new life and I must stay with it at least another year.

To settle the Mary Claybrook matter I will say that if it was not for the others and sisters that I have known I would put woman kind down as a most dismal failure whose minds abide not on one purpose and whose feet run after strange gods. I knew the beautiful and C Mary better than any of you and knowing was not so very surprised though I did think she was a superior sort of young person. Lucy's remark about the poles or rather the thought that gave it birth had been rumoring around in my brain in an unformed sort of way for a long time, something like this, Lawrence at the South Pole I at the North Pole and MC at the Middle Pole. I am as fat as a mole but am sadly deficient in hair as of old only more so. I ain't like Paw. Bald heads may be honorable, but too much honor 'tis a burden Cromwell that will sink a navy.

If I dont write enough about Chu and Brokie's kid it isn't that I forget but am so full of things I want to say that I get tired before I get to them. I hope some day to take that kid of yours under my wing and push him along.

You are right! I always knew that Jay D. had a great future as a beauty ahead of her. Her eyes were deadly to any man whose brain was satisfied entirely through his eyes.

Lovingly, Hunter

Rampart City
July 12 1899[40]

Dear Mother

Don't worry yourself about mail any more it is all coming along beautifully now. I got a letter from Father, written at Omaha May 18, a week ago and one from you written June 2, yesterday and I think things will go better after this. You can send all the newspapers of whatever kind you feel like sending. They come through now in good shape.

For what particular abomination was old Moore put in the "skookum" house?[41] I doubt the wisdom of locking those fellows up for any thing short of libel or real filth, blasphemy and that sort of thing is to be settled between the man and God and if there is no God as Moore contends then there can be no blasphemy. The more that class of fanatics is punished the more they will howl and the whole kit and bilin of em is dead anxious to pose as martyrs any how, let him go on and he hurts nobody except those who are looking for trouble.

By the way I saw the account of Moores doins in the Leader you sent me. We got thousands of old papers by the last two boats 24 mail bags full and I have been catching up on the news of the past two years.

I wrote Father a long letter about two months ago. I hope he'll get it as he and I seem to have a particularly tough time getting our correspondence running smoothly.

I think you and Father are wise to insist on Lucy's[42] staying at home this year. I always knew that she was studying entirely too hard and taking life too seriously. I told you all time and again that it would not pay no

---

40 Note in the margin: I have a standing order with you to give my love and all such salutations to Sallie Bryan and the Daingerfields and the Saunders et al I seem to be getting a lot of glory for nothing not having fought bled and died for my country. Alaska glory is [ ] as fully 30000 men have come in here, mosquitos are fat and promising. H

41 Skookum-house means "jail" in the Chinook Indian dialect.

42 Lucy Stuart Fitzhugh, Hunter's youngest sister who later became a lawyer. She was engaged to a sea captain but was jilted by him. She died in Washington Park Sanitorium, Tacoma Park, Maryland, in 1919.

Hunter's chapel looked similar to this log cabin church in Juneau.

matter how much glory and honor as a scholar she might gain,—what shall it profit a girl if she gains all the learning in the world and loses her own health. I wish she could manage to take a trip from Seattle up the inside passage to Wrangle

and Juneau it would cure anybody of anything. If I ever get money enough I am going to take that trip again and enjoy myself it is the prettiest scenery in the world I really believe.

We are having the most delightful summer, it rains every day or two and the nights are cool while the days are sunny and mild. We read until about 1 or two O K in the mornings now, never using a candle although the days have been shortening since June 21st.

Lieutenant Bell commanding this post has been ordered to Manilla [Manila] and a new set of soldiers will come in pretty soon. You never saw a more orderly town than this and we even have service every Sunday evening now. Mr. Prevost the Epis' missionary for the Yukon has put a lay reader Mr. E. J. Knapp in charge of the mission here. I suppose you have been reading about Cape Nome. Well dont believe it yet. No Cape Nomes or Cape Yes'ms either catch me in a hurry and we begin to hear very discouraging reports from there already, it is the most desolate country in the world, not a stick of timber as big as a broom stick for miles (several hundred miles) and every bit of fire wood will have to be carried by ship and then hauled six or eight miles to the diggins, while we have plenty of the best spruce and birch and nice warm gulches wherein to build our cabins. This is about the best part of Alaska and it looks from here exactly like the mountain country of Alabama. I have been eating radishes and lettuce from my garden for some time now and it is fine.

Last week I was down on our levee watching a small "Yukoner" land when two or three of its crew jumped ashore and grabbed me and almost kissed me—they were men— they called me by name and asked me about Otterson before I could get my breath. At first I couldn't divine who they were, until one of them said—"and wheres that bloody blooming dog of yours dontcherknow?" Then I was enlightened they were members of an English party with whom Otterson, Indian Dick and I stayed during a three day blizzard near the mouth of the Stickine over a year ago, in those days I had a ferocious beard and was stuffed up in winter clothes yet those fellows recognized me in spite of my having fattened 23 pounds and having no mustache or beard.

Just think I left those fellows 3000 miles away 18 months ago I going north and they stopping permanently to cut wood for steamers yet we met in the exact center of Alaska and recognized each other. They came in by the Telegraph Crk, Dease Lake, Liard River, Pelly River, Yukon route and ran out of grub for 15 days living on mush made of flour and water. Yet all are sound and healthy. Just look that route up on the map. One of my partners Ralph Dutcher left for home last week and Joe Bush and I are living together as peacefully as two doves having put two windows in our cabin and lined the walls and ceiling with pink cheese cloth.

About two thirds of our population has left us and I am glad as it gives us a better chance next winter.

This will be my last year in here in any event.

Lovingly Hunter

No 12 above Hoosier Creek
Nov 12 1899

Dear Mother

While taking dinner with Mr Prevost the Epis' minister at Rampart last Sunday I happened to look out of the cabin window and saw a big cake of ice float slowly, so slowly it was barely perceptible down the Yukon. Suddenly it stopped, wheeled slowly around then settled against the anchor ice and stopped to move no more until next May. So the Yukon died once more and now its frozen corpse is marked all over with sled trails and the tracks of dogs and men. Soon I hope the mail carrier will appear at the bend above town with his dog sled loaded with mail from the outside, but maybe it will be like last year no news until nearly spring. I was in town last Sunday getting a load of grub to bring out Monday and while I was sawing wood Mr Knapp a layman assisting Mr Prevost came down to my cabin and told me that as it was the first Sunday in the month Communion service would be held at the "chapel" so I went and never did I attend a more peculiar service, there were only three of us present Knapp, Prevost and I all by ourselves we went through the whole business from beginning to end even took up collection and got "six bits" 75 cts,—25 cts each—no chance for a hold out. When nearly at the end a little Indian boy came in and went through the service perfectly even singing "Angels and Arch angels" etc with us. It was very strange very weird and very impressive. It would astonish you to hear the Indians go through the service. Prevost has taught a few of them to read but they most of them have both words and music by heart and respond in their low rather plaintive voices in perfect time. I took dinner after church with Mr P and found him a most delightful man full of fun and anecdotes a thorough Yukoner and a splendid specimen of muscular Christianity. The church is a little 4 x 18 log cabin and the lectern is made of spruce and covered by a "fair white cloth" made by a lady who lives in town it looks like Canton flannel.

Preston and I are fixed up in elegant style our cabin is the cleanest and most home like one of the gulch we have canvas on the floor and the walls and have decorated the interior with Gibson Girls and Peter Newell monstrosities. Lucy and Evelyn's pictures adorn my side, I havent made porous plasters of them. We have two lamps and red curtains, a table cloth and a place for every thing etc. Our cache is full of good grub and take it all in all there are few people outside who are more comfortable, last winter was a nightmare this winter is a peaceful dream. We have all our winters wood down and nothing to do but dig which after all is about the easiest part of mining.

The final freeze-up of the winter came about October 1st and since then the mercury has ranged from about zero to 35degrees below 0. Today it is 26 degrees below but that conveys no idea to your mind as it is our normal winter weather and we are out in it for five or six hours without going near a fire it is just right to work. I wear only a suit of underwear and a common blue flannel shirt no furs—we only see furs in Alaska when some chu chorco fresh from the states blossoms out in a heavy fur parkie [parka] and fur leggings which he quickly throws aside when he has once followed a dog team for a few hours and finds his underclothing wet with sweat.

Tell L and E that they "done well" on Bridget but I can't send any nuggets until the river opens as the mails are closed to everything except 1st class matter.

The boys on the next claim 400 from us have been picking up good prospects every day. They have picked up—not panned—about $20000 in the last two weeks. They showed me this a m about a dozen pieces from $200 to $1200 each so our chance is very good but there is absolutely no counting on it gold is where you find it and nowhere else. I was out with a fellow for a week not long ago and I staked a claim on a new creek, but we stake in this country as we dynamite fish in the states, throw in the dynamite if any fish are within range you get if not you lose your dynamite.

To me this is the healthiest country I ever saw. I feel like a kitten all the time and never get tired. I'd just as live [lief] tackle the job of looking for the North Pole as not and if Perry or Sundrup were here, I'd go with them.

I hope Lawrence is at home. Tell him to get married but if her hame is Mary get a two years option before counting her in his assets, and let me say right here that there is very little if any blame to be laid to Mary Claybrook. I of course know many things you all know nothing about and

I find her not guilty. I didn't write as warmly as she thought I ought and I was always telling her that I would probably have to stay in here for several years. She should not have been so "suddent" thats all. Thank heavens that things are as they are.

I have been reading Prof Peck and Mrs Stetson on the woman question and I think as he does—of course—if women are to be as she wants them to be "I'll none of them." There is going to be a minstrel in town Thanksgiving gotten up by camp talent and they have begged me to be "old man." It would astonish you see what a rep' I have in camp as an all round entertainer they want me to sing nigger songs or make a speech or do any old thing. They say that every body they see tells them I am the only man for the job, even Prevost who by   the way is main guy in it and sings—he has a splendid voice "Asleep in the Klondyke Vale" has tried his best to scourge me into it but if I have a reputation for being funny I propose to keep it and not knock out its brains against such an exposition of incapacity as I would make done in burnt cork. Preston is a fine man for me to be with he is an education and has taught me—unbeknownst to him—many valuable things. He writes lots of things but I dont think much of them still they get paid for and printed thats the main thing. We have Shakespere, Browning, Longfellow, Scott, Pepy's diary, a big Websters dictionary and lots of other first class books out here to the awe and consternation of "de push on de creek."

I have finished Pan Michael and think the last half of it splendid but it is too long. Bosia is a sweet little cherub but I like not that Krysia with the maustachs [mustaches] on her lip. I am now reading "School for Saints" and may like when I get to where it is better than it is thus far.

Tell Nannie that if she has any of her poetry flying around loose Id like to get a sample or so new or old. I found that little poem about the kid that was telling his experience because he was only 7 or whatever the age was. I cut it out of an old magazine I found over on Quail Creek. Preston was quite tickled over it. Preston is in town today so I am taking things easy eating when and what I please and writing letters. Ill put this letter away now and will add to it from day to day. This is the first letter I have written for a month or so as I knew it would do as well to write all at once for no mail has left here for two months and is not likely to leave for a few days yet.

Monday, November 20th.

I'll record last week's happenings and send this letter to town by the first man going in.

I put my shaft down 6 ft a few days ago and was rejoicing at my good luck in not striking water as the rest have done when low! Then I hit one last blow with my pick when up gushed a stream of water and I barely had time to get out before it had risen to within two feet of the top so now I have four ft of solid ice to pick through when it freezes if ever it does.

John Manook the father of this camp spent Tuesday with us on his way up the creek. He is a cross between a Russian and a Yukon squaw, his name is Russian but he talks "Siwash" and looks like a nigger but is very entertaining and tells splendid stories of the Russian days in Alaska and about the first steam boat on the Yukon etc. Next day after he left Mr Knapp the N.Y. Layman who assists Mr Prevost spent the day and night with us and was very agreeable. Yesterday Messrs Sturgis and Atwood came out with 5 dogs and stayed until a few minutes ago they are both Cornell men and are nice sort of fellows. I cooked steadily all day yesterday and didnt get much rest, besides entertaining people in Alaska is very expensive when everything costs 50 cts a can and butter $100 per pound, sugar 30 cts and milk 50 cts but some day I get it back.

The boys above us still pick up nuggets they found a $15oo one last week but the water is driving them out. This is a very warm season so far we had it from 10degrees to 30degrees below up to last few days but since then it has hovered about 0 and we are praying for 50degrees to 60degrees weather so we can work.

We all have a great curiosity to know what we are doing in the Phillipines but our wires are down so will have to wait for the mail. I have my bread in the oven now and must needs go and tend it.

Sunday, November 26th.

How fast the weeks do fly in this country especially in winter. The days are only 6 hours long now and this time next month they will be only a little

A panoramic view of Rampart City from the banks of the Yukon, 1899.
The mission chapel Hunter attended can be seen on the right of the small
white building in the center.

over four hours long so as we put in such a big part of our time sleeping and reading the winter flies by "ere we're aware" and nothing to show for it. The sun poked his face up through a crack at the end of the gulch November 14 and has not been seen since and will not see it until about February 1st 00.

We had another guest a day or two ago Mr. Knapp (not E J who stayed with us before, but the magistrate of Rampart District). Preston and I will go in town next Thursday, Thanksgiving day to Jollify and see the minstrels.

It is really unpleasantly warm nowadays it has ranged between zero and 10degrees for the past two weeks it is too warm to mine as our fires burn too much unless it is about 25degrees or 30degrees below and then a fellow gets too warm working hard any how and it is almost impossible to keep our cabins cool enough and keep any fire at all. We have to keep the door open nearly all the time. I am now sitting in the cabin in my underclothes and am rather too warm. None of us wear more than two shirts anyway. We are not comfortable with the thermometer above 15 degrees below. I'll add some over time.

Rampart
Nov 30

This is the last supplement to my continued letter as the mail will leave for the outside before I could send in a letter from the creek.

The minstrel last night was a surprisingly good performance as good as the average "outside" regular minstrels but that is no great compliment to the Rampart boys. The local hits and the singing was really first class. There were about 200 people present at $2oo per head the show wound up with a big dance and free lunch.

You can see by the "walk and conversation" of the men on the streets that things are going well on the creeks. They have struck it all the way from "good" to rich on Little Manook, Little Manook Jr, Eureka and Hoosier— my creek but the latter owing to this beastly warm spell of weather is full of water so we cant get to bed rock.

I enclose a piece of poetry gotten up by Preston on an idea I gave him. The drawing I found on the trail. There is all kinds of talent in this town when you hunt for it.

I wish I could report a good strike on my own account but my time hasn't come yet. "Nemine" it only takes one day and one letter to make me O.K. When bed rock shows up I may make a good stake, and if I dont I've lived that long anyhow, and will probably be no worse off than I would be in the states.

I hope Lawrence is home now. I enjoyed his letter. Tell him to do it again.

Lovingly, Hunter

Thermometer 15 degrees

Dec 17[43]

Yesterday, Sunday Preston went to town, and Mr Koonce—the parson and I held down the house alone. Late in the p m he and I went over to the Granite State boys' cabin and "had church." It was rather a dismall performance as there were only seven of us including the Parson and me. The five Granite State boys had to be "old man" because they found it too cold to lie out in the timber in 3 ft. of snow but next time I think they will take the snow. Verily it was a case of two or three being gathered together.

Koonce and I had a long discussion on the subject of the translation of the Bible and Hebrew in general. I wouldnt be a preacher for the richest paystreak in Alaska.

Dec 18

Mr. Koonce left this a m I am glad to say this thing of cooking for three days hand running for a stranger makes me tired and then its so blamed hard to think what to have for the next meal, but for dinner yesterday I gave him, corn, peas, roast mutton, and potatoes, and for dessert ginger snaps and cornstarch pudding-also cocoa. This morning I filled him up on crystallized eggs, Buckwheat cakes and maple syrup, thank heavens tomorrow Preston cooks!

I had to clean out my own hole today going down and filing the bucket and then climbing up and hoisting out. It was tiresome but not so bad. The mercury fell to 45degrees bellow 0 last night and is getting [colder] tonight. Preston got back.

Dec 19

We didn't get up until 9:30 this a m because it is so dark at that hour that we can't tell how late it is. Our alarm clock went back on us a day or two ago and we are helpless. I wonder why things that ought to do things never do things when they are most needed, it is a curse to be born with the sort of temperament that requires sleep in the morning when others are

---

43   1899

getting up, but thats the way I'm constituted. Getting up in the morning is now and ever was the hardest thing to discipline myself to. I can sit up all night and enjoy it. I can go two days without eating and feel OK. I can travel 40 miles in a day and feel fine at night. I can stand the severest cold and most deadly heat and even mosquitos dont phase me but when it comes to getting up before I am "good and ready" I am a poor lost and undone creature, too low down in spirits to call my soul mine own.

Nothing new today except that I'll put on two pairs of moccasins tomorrow if this wind keeps up. I nearly lost that last year's toe of mine at the windlass today. Anyway you take it windlassing sho is a cold job.

Next Monday is Xmas just think—15 years ago I would have been wild with excitement but now how tame even sad the old landmark seems and the day after I'll be 30 and only last week I was 20. Oh well! it'll be all the same in a hundred years.

Dec 21

As nothing of importance happened yesterday I did not write up this diary but will record the few incidents that marked the day.

When Preston came from town he brought me two Ptarmigan sent me by Doc Hudgin Yesterday I baked them with bread stuffing and they were fine. Late in the p m Jack Welsh and Hort Smith dropped in to borrow books. They had neither found any thing in the way of prospects worthy of note. I am getting tired of this working for nothing and will look out for something more profitable when I go to town.

Dec 21 Shortest day in the year we only have 5 hours of so called daylight now and it is rather gloomy. The thermometer registered 50 degrees below today and is about that now. Our holes were pretty well frozen up this a m so we didnt do much in them. Preston and I dont get along as well as two little doves, he knows it all and so do I, and then the work on this claim seems to be a blank anyhow. The reports from Little Manook Jr make me desperate. Why does the gold always come so near me and not near enough for me to get it. I dunno maybe tis Kismet. Id like to be at home tonight.

Dec 24

Xmas Eve but it doesn't seem like it.

Yesterday Preston and I after hoisting out one hole came to town in spite of a temperature of 60 below but the lower the better for me, if I could walk every day 8 miles in a 60 below 0 climate I'd live forever.

The first thing after getting to town I made 15 pounds of candy for Doc. Hudgin for Xmas display.

I stayed with Drake last night and got up at 1130 a m the fashionable hour in town. Today I made some more candy Lemon drops Peppermint drops and sticks and pop corn balls. I cook so much on Sunday anyway that making candy comes naturally, thus do we go back on ourselves on the Yukon.

It is almost impossible to believe that this is that greatest of all nights Xmas Eve, when I used to go to bed clothes and all and lie awake 10 minutes thinking it was so many hours and then suddenly wake up realizing it was Xmas Day, out I'd tumble "all standing" and dash madly for my stocking.

But after all there is not such a difference between then and now, in fact there are points of resemblance. I go to bed all standing and dont go to sleep as soon as I would like, when [in] the morning I eagerly look into my socks to see what the mice have brought me, and I always find split peas, dried potatoes, rice chips etc

I forgot to say that last night I went to a squaw dance and we had a hot time there were about two dozen squaws there and they danced every kind of dance and some of them are really graceful waltzers one of the girls gracefully draped herself over her partners arm like some of these would be lissome society girls do outside. All the society girls danced Lucy Baggage, Scar faced Ellen, short and dirty, Thomsons Maggie, and the whole list, dressed in all sorts and conditions of clothes, calico dresses, silk dresses, all kinds of dresses, mucklucks, moose moccasins, wolves mazinkas and now and then a pair of outside shoes. The boys were dressed just as they work on the gulches, mucklucks, parkas and all. I'd give anything if I could have some people up here whom I know—or some people whom I know up here, during some of our social performances.

I was talking to old Capt. Mayo today. Capt. is a smart fine old fellow.

He has been on the Yukon since 1868, never having been outside since. He has read a great deal and talks of the latest discoveries of science etc., but he has never seen any electric appliance except the lights on the steamers. He has a squaw for a wife and a dozen or so beautiful children.[44] He told me of a curious coincidence that happened partly during the war in—63 and partly in Alaska in 98, he divided his rations while with Sherman at Macon Ga with a negro who was about starved and last year an old negro whom we all know here, went up to Capt Mayo and told him that he looked like a man who fed him during the war etc. Wasnt that queer?

Christmas Day—45 degrees

I got up at 11:30 a m and had buckwheat cakes and cocoa for breakfast. I quit using coffee a year ago. Most of the boys are in from the gulches and all look happy and prosperous. One of them picked up a $1000oo within the last few weeks and a good many nuggets ranging from $10oo to $75oo have been found.

I went to church last night and heard a good sermon; tonight I go to the "show" given by the Masons. Tonight and tomorrow—my 30th birthday—we go out to Hoosier to worm our way into the secrets of the earth.

The camp is far more cheerful and prosperous than last Xmas.

I took dinner with Preston at the restaurant and had oyster cocktail, soup, lobster salad, green peas, fresh potatoes, moose steak, roasted Ptarmigan, plum pudding, and ice cream, all for $1oo, which is cheap enough for anybody.

I'll write up the show tomorrow and then close this letter.

Note: There are possibly two pages missing here. This was evidenced by Fitzhugh's page numbers.

---

44   Copy of original letter is illegible, and Mrs. Smith's transcription has been relied upon.

Dec 26

I am 30 today and feel just like I did yesterday. The show last night was splendid and everybody was in a gloriously hilarious mood. Mrs Wiggins sang and recited and was encored ferociously her "How Ole Folks Won the Oaks" was a perfect joy to the boys the Little Manook Quartette dressed in their mining clothes—they were pressed into service without notice and the "pay stain" on their clothes delighted the crowd. The Rampart Guitar and Mandolin "Club" was far better than most outside concerns of the kind. Mr Prevost—the Episcopal Minister sang "Finiculi Finicule" and did it well. The audience was enthusiastic all through, but I was sitting 6 ft from a red hot stove my back burning up and my moccasins frozen hard and fast to the floor so that I nearly pulled them off when I moved. (Capt Mayo sang a good original comic song.)[45]

We went to bed at 4 p m so we concluded to stay in town another day, also to celebrate my birthday etc.

This finishes this document. I can only add that I am on the trail of several more claims, and maybe one of them will turn out pretty good. I am glad Xmas is gone for after all it has a yellow streak through it these days.

I may make enough of a stake this winter and spring to keep me at home for awhile next year. So may it be!

You are mighty good about writing to me. Keep it up.

Lovingly Hunter

---

45 Mrs. Smith's transcription has been relied upon for several words in the sentences in this letter.

FRAGMENT OF LETTER[46]

January 9, 1900

. . . awfully afraid of water as one of my holes has already filled up and the boys next door have five holes to bed rock and all are filled with water making the work of 6 men for two months as nothing. I really think we will lose our work as only one fill is necessary to fill our pay shaft with water and then we'll have it all to do over again in which event I'll pack my sled with all my worldly goods and drag my slow length along to town and look for another job at wages, thats the way with us fellows we never know where we're at.

The boys on Little Manook Jr have it rich, only 20 ft to bed rock, no water, 5 feet of pay, 20 ft wide and running from 10 cts to $11.00 to the pan i.e. two shovels full or two shovel fulls whichever it is. They find small nuggets right along, about 4 or 5 dollars being common. The biggest nugget on this creek so far was found on No 17 above. It went $27oo at 18 per oz. The record for this season so far is with Little Manook several lumps between $10oo and $30oo being found and one weighing $76oo was found at the dump on No 8 above.

This thing of placer mining is fascinating after all for a man never knows when he is going to pick up the largest nugget in the world. I may find it tomorrow and I probably will not find more than a few cents and I am likely to find our shaft full of water.

I am always telling my partner, George Hyde Preston (he likes all this name), that it would fill me with joy just to be able to turn a lot of girls I know loose on our dump and tell them they could have all they can pick up it would be worth the price to see the fun. I picked up over $7oo on another fellows dump yesterday in less than half an hour.

I enclose a small color, or rather a large color or small nugget. It weighs 7 1/2 grains and as gold at $18oo per oz is worth 90 cts per part or 3 3/4 cents per grain as the Pirates of Penzance hath it, "By a simple arithmetical

---

46   The manuscript begins with page 3. Apparently it was written to someone other than a menber of Fitzhugh's immediate family.

process you will easily discover" that this piece of gold is worth the whole sum of 28 cents. I send you this because it doesnt cost me much and it serves to show you what we look for in this country, if every pan had one of these in it I would be a millionaire—but its good ground that will show up a 28 cent piece in 5 pans and most claims in this country dont give more than a cent per pan, though several in this district are very good. I will say right here that Uncle Sam will not allow us to send anything bulky or scratchy through the mails in Alaska hence I have to send you a very flat, very small nugget, and its glad I am that our postal regulations make sending an ounce nugget an impossibility, for now I have an excuse for sending colors.

My wrist is "drefful" painful and writing is a hard job for me these days so you can just give me credit for being very nice, etc. for writing while in this condition but I didnt tell you what the condition was, did I? Well I was down in my tunnel a few days ago picking away when a big boulder fell and nearly cracked my skull—no jokes please—I threw one hand up and steered the stone away from my head but the strain was too much for my "lily white" and it sprained my wrist, but I have been working ever since odd jobs and windlassing.

Preston says he is hungry so as it is my day to cook I'll have to lay this aside.

Well I cooked some canned turkey, peas, and potatoes and made a big baked custard and tea and Preston is washing the dishes. Thats how we work it, one day I cook and do no other house work, and Preston cuts the wood, goes down to the water hole after water and washes dishes, next day the thing is reversed. I'll have to bake bread day after tomorrow and next week Preston will bake, its the way we all do in Alaska.

By the way—and I am afraid you'll be vexed but I'll venture—why do you write such an all fired fine hand that I cant read it, honest! I really cant make out some sentences at all and it is such a great disaster for a Yukoner not to be able—my wrist is playing out—to read every word of the precious letters that come to him. I took the liberty of showing Preston one sentence of your last letter for I really was desirous of acquainting myself with your meaning but he actually could do nothing with it, and he is a lawyer too. So he took up his pencil and proceeded to write a poem called "In reply to

Her Letter," all about hieroglyphics and sich like. He sent it to Life but it may not get there as[47] lots of our letters get lost in the shuffle. But if it does it will be published. He was too much inspired to make a miss and then they generally take his little poems, signed George Hyde.

Seventy reindeer came through last week on their way to Tanana River. They will haul the mail this winter.[48]

I spent last Sunday night alone in snow 4 feet deep, a mile or so from a [ ], just to "jump" a claim on the stroke of midnight, the thermometer stood at 56degrees below zero "And the hungry stars in heaven gazed like eyes of walrus upon me." At 30 seconds after 12 o'clock, January 1, 1900, I chopped a blaze on the frozen tree and straightway became owner of another claim. The coldest weather this winter was 66degrees below 0. It is 48 below now.

Pages 11–14 of the manuscript are missing. The transcript continues on the following pages.

Jan 9

I am writing in a serial sort of a way you see, a way much affected by me these days. Well I told you that I was going to find a big nugget or nothing yesterday, and I found nothing, but this a m I found $765 on the dump and a nugget of $5oo and the balance small pieces. The boys next to us found the record nugget of the creek today $5050. It is a beauty about two inches long, 1 inch broad and about 1/8 inch thick. They (the Granite State boys) found about $25oo in small pieces besides.

We hear that there is a mail in town from the outside, but it is a very small one as the mail boat was capsized on 30 Mile River and 24 out of 25 bags of mail was lost forever so I don't expect anything. We people in here have every sort of bad luck the flesh is heir to, but never mind we'll "get thar" some day.

---

47   to

48   The copy of original is illegible, and the transcription of Mrs. Smith has been relied upon.

I may add another page or two to this before I go in Saturday for a load of grub.

Rampart City
Jan 13

I'll just add this last entry and then give the whole thing to Uncle Sam to carry for me.

I found one dollar today, 300 yesterday and 300 day before on the dump. You understand that what we pick up is nothing to what is in the dump, the small gold which is the best is so covered with mud that it cannot be seen at a glance like the nuggets, but in the spring when we clean up we will get this all in the sluice boxes.

I came in to town this p m and will stay until Monday. I came in for grub but will go to church to-morrow night. We have a fine Epis' minister here Mr Prevost who has been in for 13 years.

Well tell my folks that I am writing home by this same mail, so they will be happy.[49] Love to everybody.

Yours
Hunter Fitzhugh

Prospectors mining with sluice boxes, 1905.

49   This segment appeared to be fragmented as though there are many missing pages.

Hoosier Creek
March 2 1900

Dear Mother

This will probably be the last letter you will get from me before the ice breaks up as that is what the mail carriers say—one more mail over the ice. I havent anything of importance to write. I am no better off and thank heavens no worse off than I was at the last writing.

Our pay hole—or the one from which we got what we got—filled with water last week so we have gotten nothing since except $9oo I found in a hole I sunk at a venture across the creek. This hole and another which we have nearly to bed rock may bring us in a little pay before the thaw. The boys next door found $94oo nugget not long ago it looks remarkably like an old run down at the heel brogan.

The last mail—two weeks ago brought me only two letters, both from Alabama. Della Dryer and Fannie Fitzhugh, the first I've heard from either for 3 years. Lizzie has a boy two years old—William Byrd Fitzhugh.

Front Street, Dawson, Canada 1900.

An overland bicycle record, five days from White Horse to Dawson, was set in the winter of 1903.

You would be amused at the fellows who come down from Dawson bound for Cape Nome. They come at the rate of about 20 a day with all sorts of rigs but mostly with dog sleds. Its only a short 1500 mile jaunt you know. Two fellows came down without even blankets, no grub, no stove, nothing but foot wear and an axe. Some people call them gritty but I know a name for them that is far more applicable. They trusted to stopping with wood cutters, prospectors etc. along and the merciful Providence that looks after drunkards, babies and idiots has steered them this far in safety.

Another fellow came down yesterday on a "bike". He brought his wheel up from the states by steamer and had it hauled to Lake Bennet by the railroad. From that point he rode—"all unarmed, he rode all alone" his tires were wrapped with canvas and he seemed to be doing first rate when he got to Rampart having made 800 miles in 11 days and only travelled a few hours per day, but he's another shining mark for the Fool Killer. These "Nomads" (good (pun) bring us news from the outside much later than our mail as they have a wire in to Dawson now you know. We have just heard of the death of Gen'l Roberts son in the Transvaal, I am full [of] curiosity as to the outcome of that scrap. I cant believe that England will be defeated, yet we have our 4th of July.

At last I got a letter from Sister which I at once answered. I was awfully glad to hear from her. If Lawrence is at home tell him to write to me please.

You people dont know how hard it is for us fellows up here to write. It takes a lot of will power and general goodness to work with a pick and shovel all day in a cramped up hole and then put in an hour or two writing letters at night. Its nearly 10 oclock now and I've got to take a bath for I am going to town tomorrow and besides that I've got to go down in my shaft and light my fire tonight so you see its something of a job for a Yukoner to write letters.

I never heard of my Jap after I left Dawson. Then he was at Telegraph.

I wrote Brokie a long letter about her new one. Gee whiz! but I am getting behind the times. We have beautiful brilliant sunshine now from 9:30 to 2 p m and it makes us all feel like young unicorns. Father says you are not in good health nowadays. I hope its only one of those common ailment spells you always had.

Good night Hunter

Rampart, Alaska
July 5 1900

Dear Father

I enclose you with this an "expurgated edition" of a letter to me from my old hunting and rustling partner Otto Kroehle of Cleveland, Ohio. It is a thoroughly characteristic and satisfactory letter and I'll bet my last cent on its reliability. Otto grew somewhat sore on this camp before he left and begged me to go down to Nome with him over the ice but the ray of light that shone on his mental vision was spotted with motes of doubt ere it reached me so I declined. He is a fellow who is as honest and industrious as a man can be but lacks that great element of sticktoitiveness, if when we go fishing he fails to get a "rise" at the first pool he at once grows weary of the whole enterprise and wants to go back to town but when he lands a fish he begins to plan for a long stay and talks of putting up fish for the market etc. Well he has just landed a big trout now. I'd like to have heard him just before the rise. I got back from a 16 days stay in the mountains about 30 miles from here. I was absolutely alone except for my good old dog "Sport"—may he never grow lean. There was a mountain rising just above my camp—my permanent camp—about 9000 ft high and I was prospecting about it and frequently went up to the very summit where the black volcanic rock stands on end like old Druidical temples. The view was something grand. I could see 200 miles of the Yukon and about 150 miles of the Tanana Rivers. Mount McKinley supposed now to be the highest point in the N A continent probably 26000 ft high stood out boldly in relief 125 miles to the south. Mounts Haynes, Wrangel and a lot of smaller ones all snow clad on the summits and glistening with glaciers lower down "lined up" along the southern horizon like a big white washed back fence. If the mosquitos would only let us alone this would be a beautiful country in summer but the fiends torment us all the time even on the summit of Wolverine Mountain they were terrible—oh! well its no use [to] write about them I could never do them justice.

Yesterday was the glorious 4th but it was very mild here as we havent over 100 people in town and they are not of the noisy kind. I made a lot

Rampart City, Alaska, 1897

of candy and rigged my sail boat preparatory to going up the River tomorrow—if the wind is fair. Doctor Hudgin and I have a wood yard and "coal mine" about 12 miles up the Yukon and I am going up to prospect the coal seam as well as to sell the wood to steamboats at $10oo per cord. An Indian has just left me who came to see if he could go up with me as he has a salmon camp a few hundred feet from my cabin. I like to be near the Indians. They are good neighbors and are always finding something queer in the way of fish or animals—I mean flesh. The salmon are running now and I saw an Indian woman catch two fish yesterday one 45 lb and one 25 lb. I will set a net too and catch a lot this summer.

Bear are very plentiful now. I saw the track of a big savage cinnamon last week but I couldnt trail him over the dry rock so lost him. Moose and caribou are getting into the low grounds now so as to stand in the lakes and rivers and fight mosquitos all day long.

I caught an old hen Ptarmigan and four little chickens over on quail and brought them alive 25 miles although I had to carry them in my hat and go bare headed all that distance over the mountains and through swamps and besides my head is as barren of hair as a base ball as I had singed my few hairs off. Any how I got them all to town safely but they all died in captivity. The little ones look exactly like these little stupid ground squirrel chickens that turn into great clumsy footed raucous voiced "yaller" hens in the fullness of time. The old ones are brown now and full of all kinds of schemes for luring you away from their young. Alas! poor things. Nature didnt seem to count on the wondrous intelligence of man who refusing to follow the broken winged mother grabs the little fluffy yellow chicks and let them die slowly.

We all have great hopes that something will be struck on the high bars in this district this summer and if there is all of the few who are here will have a pull at it. Im getting a little tired of waiting for fortune to point her finger at me and say Ne-e-ext! but it may come after all.

I cant realize that there is any politics we have nothing to do with it here, but from the way my letters and those of my friends sound I believe that Bryan[50] is the man. The trouble is that his non-Imperialism doesnt fit the West and his free silver doenst dovetail with the East. Most of my friends here are western men and they all seem to be Bryan men. I got a letter from you written from the neighborhood of Pikes Peak. Do it again.

Your loving son, Hunter

---

50 William Jennings Bryan was nominated by the Populist Party and ran for President of the United States in 1900. He took a strong stand for free and unlimited coinage of silver as a means to economic recovery. He lost the election to Republican William Mckinley.

Rampart, Alaska
Aug 1st 1900

Dear Mother

I don't feel as much like writing a letter as I might in fact writing is always hard to do in this country where a man has all his own housework to do as well as his outside work.

I have been up the river for the past 4 weeks living entirely alone. At first there was an Indian camp about a mile each way from me but they all got sick at once and the more I doctored the sicker they got so I hustled the whole "shooting match" down town to Dr Hudgin they had grip and pleurisy. There has been a wide spread but mild wave of grip over the length of the Yukon valley.

I have lived entirely alone with no human being within 15 miles for about two months and I dont like it. It makes a person gloomy and I find myself talking to myself in a loud key all the time. They say that that is a sign a man is getting nutty.

I have gotten letters from you, Father, Evelyn, and Brokie within the last month. A letter from Father dated June 28th was received July 27th and was particularly welcome as it backed me up in my determination to stay another season in here if I cant get out before without losing what hold I have on the country.

It doesnt seem to occur to you people at home that I would give anything to go home. I wouldnt need any word of begging if I could find any way to get home in any thing like good shape. It's hard to stay up here so long but if there is any thing in this life that isnt hard I'd like to see it. If I were to go home now I'd be a disagreeable dejected seedy looking man in a very few weeks. I know myself well enough for that. Many a man has stayed away from home as long as I have. It's nothing uncommon.

A big strike was made on Slate Creek last week. I have a claim on the creek but I am entirely too far up to run any chance of getting any thing I think.

We expect quite a crowd in here this Fall from down the River the Cape Nome bubble has "busted" just as I said it would and the idiots who left good outfits and comfortable cabins here to go down there are coming back

"Soapy" Smith's saloon in Skaguay [sic], Alaska, 1898.

strapped and dismal. Small pox was pretty bad down there but is about done now we hear.

I have been catching a great many salmon up the river. Every day I go up to my nets and take out from 3 to 10 salmon weighing between 12 and 30 lbs. I am drying them for dog feed next winter. You would enjoy the beautiful long red steaks from the king salmon, sometimes 16 inches long and six inches wide and one inch thick without skin or bone but I am sick of it and throw them to the dog. Fish dont do for a steady diet with me.

I am glad to hear that Smith has been promoted to a place in Augusta Ga but I am not surprised he is a thorough going steady business man and has no reason to do anything but rise.

Did I ever tell you about my debut as a professional musician? Any how Ill tell it again it is not much to tell but shows how devious are the ways of him that seeketh a grub stake; we have here several musicians, but one expert a Mr Fleischman a San Francisco Jew he is a violinist of the first rank in S.F. but is a PM [Past Master] here. He plays for all the dances here and is much in demand. He usual [usually] gets another fellow to play guitar for him at these dances. Well about two months ago he came to me and asked me to play the guitar for him that night at a squaw dance at the Miner Saloon (almost all the dances are in saloons here). I told him that I didnt think I could hold down the job but he said I could play loud where I was sure I was right and just go through a pantomime when I was "lost." So that night I played for three solid hours on an old door supported on whiskey bbls as a platform. The room was full of squaws and strangers from Dawson and the tobacco smoke was so thick you could cut it but I went through the motions all the time. Sometimes I played and sometimes I didnt, for Fleishman just made that old fiddle hum and played an endless medley. After the dance the "bar keep" gave me a five dollar bill and thanked me most kindly.

I cant write any more. Ive too many other letters.

Yours, Hunter

The last letter my precious boy wrote me. It is dated just six days before the Lord took him.51

Rampart
Oct 29 1900

Dear Mother

I don't know how long it has been since I wrote to you last or when I heard from you. I hope the cause of your silence is due to our awful mail service as I don't hear from anybody at all. The mails this summer have been far worse than those of last winter. The trouble is we poor expatriated cusses up here have no vote hence any thing is good enough for us but wait until we are a great state and then we likewise will have our good things mail service and all the rest of it.

Well this winter I will at last work my own property. I have claim No 31 and will have a fourth interest in claims 22 and 23 on Slate Creek of which I have written you in times past. My "pardner" this year is an old man about 50 but white haired and fat he is from a little country neighborhood in NY state, is named Drake and is a good worker a shrewd Yankee and has no nerves to bother so I think we will make it O K, if we strike it this winter I may go home next year a bonanza king Quien Sabe?

Slate Creek is (the mouth of it) 12 miles up Big Manook but we have to go up the creek about 4 miles to our cabin making a 16 mile trip to town but that is nothing in the winter over 12 miles of smooth creek trail and 4 miles of pretty "tolerble" decent side hill and "glacier" creek trail. I have been out in the hills for the past four weeks prospecting and building a cabin. Oh! this eternal round of cabin building when will it end! I and another fellow—a Morman from Utah—whipsawed 600 ft of lumber last week for our floor, door and windows. The Yukoners say that when one of us who has not been as good as he should be dies the devil puts him to whipsawing but if he is faithful and doesn't complain under the trial he is

---

51   Note added by Agnes M. Fitzhugh

Panning for gold on the Yukon River downstream from Rampart.

then simply burned through eternity like an ordinary goat of the left hand well it is trying, this thing of making a saw mill of yourself. I killed a great many Ptarmigan this fall one day I went up into the high "Alpine meadows of snow" and in two hours killed 27 birds with my 22 cal rifle. Tell Lawrence if he wants to know anything about 22s just call on me. I am the greatest authority in this country having used all kinds of them and every variety of ammunition. I took my 30-30 and went after a band of caribou one day last week but when I got up among the peaks a gale second in severity to none I ever saw drove me down just as I had struck their sign. The wind picked up chunks and slabs of hard snow and simply drove me to cover in the valley. I was as I usually am in my shirt sleeves and it was the first time a blizzard drove me from the field but I had to fall back. You cannot possibly conceive what these mountains are in the winter time—it has been winter for a month.

I believe I wrote some of you of our new girl Miss Gonott. Well "she's a beaut" and all the boys are sprucing up in great shape for her benefit. I put on a white collar—the first one since leaving Seattle in 98—and went to a real nice whist party and dance a few weeks ago and some sort of festivity is going on nearly every night now and I am a great society man but we fellows on the gulches have to dig and hoist and pan and chop and cook and sew and toil and moil and sweat and swear all winter while the fellows in town rush the girls and wear felt shoes and don't get their noses frozen so they look nice and the girls—or girl— think they are so nice while they think we are good worthy young men but smell a trifle too much of burnt wood and have rather hard hands and walk a little too stiff legged.

We have had a paper for some time now The Alaska Forum it is about as big as two stamps stuck together on one edge and the Editor has had two fights already for being to [too] fearless (?) and too unsparing in the use of the mighty power of the press.

Did I answer Brokie's letter and picture, if no say to her that I was "ever so tickled" to get them and people admire her picture like the dickens. I wish you folks would all send me pictures. I have Lucy's and Es [Evelyn's] and Bs [Brokie's] standing on my set of "Muhlbachs" and would like best

Whipsawing: "It's a hard craft."

in the world to add all the balance of yez Lawrence as well as the girls and you and Pa.

By the way if you can, get the new Yukon novel, "The Son of the Wolf."[52] I just glanced through it today for the first time and the fellow who owns it says he will lend it to me when about two dozen others have read it so it looks like I will not get a chance to read it carefully but I can see that it is an A 1 sketch of our life up here. The dog talk, the descriptions of our costumes and all the stage settings and business are just as I would have put had I been able to write. The Indian talk is a little off color as he makes them use too much Chinook of which they are entirely ignorant. I can lay it all over him in "taking off the Lemoshi." The frontis piece is particularly good. Note the different kinds of foot gear and clothing. The ice began to run October 9th and is still running but will probably freeze up in a few days.

Be sure to send clippings and dont forget the election. Goodnight

Your loving son Hunter

---

52 Written by Jack London

Hunter's Death

Rampart, Alaska
Nov. 12, 1900

Dear Mrs. Fitzhugh

Your son and I lived together all last winter, and I am writing this not only because I want to tell you how deep is my sympathy with you in your grief, but also because I want you to know how he had endeared himself to me, and how sadly I feel his loss and what a grief it is to me.

He spoke so often of you all in our talks in the cabin during the long winter evenings that I almost feel that I know you and I cannot feel a stranger to the family of one who was so true a friend to me. He was always cheery and hopeful, and brightened many hours for me that would otherwise have been dreary ones.

I need not tell you of his high sense of honor. He was incapable of a mean action, and he was always unselfish and thoughtful of others. In the last talk I had with him he was making suggestions that he thought might help me in working my claim, and the very men who are on the claim now were, I know, influenced to come by what he said to them, although he never mentioned to me that the had spoken to them.

He was very ingenious, and while we were on the claim he always had some neighbor's clock or something of that kind that he was mending for him. These are little things, perhaps, but they show the nature of a man I know of no better way to describe him than to say he was one who was always doing something for some body else.

Removing the body of an avalanche victim (not Hunter) at Chilkoot Pass.

I know how very hard it is for you that he died so far away from you all and from his home, but I want you to feel and to be assured that everything that could be done was done by sorrowing, loving friends, who grieve with you and whose hearts go out to you in deepest sympathy.

Most sincerely yours,

George H. Preston

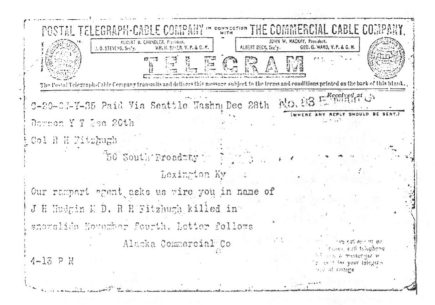

Telegram sent to Hunter's father informing him of his son's death.

The Alaska Commercial Company buildings at Rampart.

St. Andrew's Mission Rampart, Alaska
Nov. 12, 1900

Dear Mrs. Fitzhugh,

You will learn through letters written by others the sad details of the death of your son, Robert H. Fitzhugh, which has brought sorrow to the hearts of his many friends in this community, and to myself a sense of personal loss which is indeed very great. They will tell you how he perished in a snow slide on a mountain while hunting. But I want to let you know something about our friendship for each other, which was to be one of the brightest experiences I have enjoyed since coming to this country in which there is so much that is dark and sombre.

I first met your son a little over a year ago, soon after I came here from New York to work as a lay missionary under Bishop Rowe, and the friendship which we then formed for each other I hoped would be one of long duration. It brought me much that cheered and encouraged me in my work, and I hope and believe that it helped to cheer him also. Your son's disposition was one of the brightest and sunniest; even in the midst of many discouraging experiences he had a high courage that was altogether admirable. He had a keen love for all that was noble and good and true and was fearless in expressing his aversion for whatever was the reverse. He loved the the beautiful in nature and had a feeling of sympathy for the young which made it easy for him to gain the friendship and devotion of children. He was unselfish and would go out of his way to do one a kindness. He loved his family and home and would often speak of them, and, best of all, he was a Christian man and was one of the few men in camp here who attended the services of the church regularly and who, when the opportunity offered, came to the Holy Communion in obedience to our Lord's command, "Do this in remembrance of me."

For some time I had been looking forward to introducing your son to the Bishop, who will soon visit me here and was expecting that he would again embrace the opportunity of coming to the Lord's Supper, little thinking that when the Bishop came he would be in Paradise.

Your son always took an active interest in the work of the Mission. Some time ago he helped me do some work toward improving the appearance of the interior of the chapel, and with his own hands he built a little closet in one corner of the chapel, which I use as a vestry room. On another occasion he came to the mission and during two days cooked for and nursed several patients who were ill in the hospital, in order to give me the opportunity to transact some business which I had with the United States District Court when it visited Rampart last summer.

Being quite alone here in the work except for the assistance given by a little half-breed Indian boy who lives with me at the mission, the help which your son gave me from time to time was valuable and very much appreciated. He was a noble, high-souled fellow, and I shall miss him very much.

In connection with your son's funeral, I want to assure you that everything was done with the utmost degree of decorum and reverence. The body was brought to the hospital of our mission on Friday, November 9, where other friends besides myself watched by it and performed the last sad offices for it. The body was embalmed, I enclose a photograph of the hospital, which is the long building on the hilltop. Your son used often to come to see me in the adjoining cabin shown in the picture and situated at right angles to the hospital building. He spent the greater part of Sunday afternoon, October 28, with me in it. On Sunday Morning, November 11, yesterday, the coffin was removed to the chapel, of which I also enclose a photograph. This is the chapel in which your son did the work which I have mentioned above. It is a small building, and in order to accommodate the people I removed several of the benches from it so as to afford plenty of standing room. A large number of people, both Indians and whites, attended the services, which of course I conducted according to the ritual of our church. The hymns "Abide With Me, Fast Falls the Eventide," "Jesus Lover of My Soul," and "Asleep in Jesus," were sung by a choir of four voices. Several friends sent wreaths of evergreens. The coffin was taken to the cemetery on a sled drawn by a dog team, and a large number of men followed it. I read the commital service at the grave. It would gratify you had I space to mention all the little things that so many people did out of their friendship and love for your son in connection with his funeral.

You will, I trust, excuse this long letter. But, I have written it, feeling that it would be a source of comfort to you to learn of the blameless, beautiful life which your son led and of the esteem in which he was held by the people and that everything was done by them that could be done in order to show their respect and love for him.

Dr. J. H. Hudgin, who for a long time was your son's mining partner, mourns the death of your son as he would that of a near relative. He is a very gentle, lovable sort of a man and is universally liked here. Mr. George H. Preston, with whom also your son was associated in certain mining operations last winter, asks me to hand you the enclosed letter.

I want to assure you, my dear Mr. and Mrs. Fitzhugh, of my heartfelt sympathy for you and all the members of your family in this great sorrow which God has sent to you, and I pray God to give you grace and strength to endure it with Christian fortitude and in the confident belief that nothing can separate you from God's love.

Yours very sincerely,

Edward J. Knapp

Mr. Drake's Letter[53]

Rampart, Alaska
Nov. 13, 1900

Mr. R. H. Fitzhugh and Family
No. 50 South Broadway
Lexington, Ky.

Dear Friends:

As I feel that I must call you under the circumstances, as your son, R. H. Fitzhugh, was a personal friend of mine. This is one of the most painful tasks that has ever fallen upon me to inform you of your son's sudden death. While he was not on the creek with me, I will try to give you as minute a detail of the circumstances connected with his death and burial as possible as I know how anxious you will be to know all. Mr. Fitzhugh and myself were partners for this winter's work and had some interests in common in other claims aside from the one that we were going to work up this winter; I had put up a cabin on my claim No. 25 above on Slate Creek in the Rampart mining district about 16 miles from Rampart, and Fitzhugh had come out with me and helped finish up the cabin October 31. We were living in a small cabin on No. 26 above while working on No. 25, and upon the night of November 3, I said to Fitzhugh now that the cabin is ready to move in, I will move in tomorrow and you may go out and locate where there is some birds in the mountains. That pleased him, as we were both fond of shooting, and upon the morning of the 4th, Fitzhugh, or as every one was in the habit of calling him Fitz—started out about 8:30 a. m. and that was the last that I ever saw him alive. I moved down into our cabin and had dinner ready at about 4 p. m., which is dark at that hour of the

---

53 Fragment of a letter as it appeared in one of the Lexington newspapers

day. When Fitz went away in the morning I asked him what time he would be back and his reply was about half-past one if he did not find the birds thick, and if he did find them thick he would not come so early. However, when it began to grow dark I began to go out and listen for him and call to see if I could get an answer and also fired off my gun, thinking that were he in hearing he would reply in like manner. But I could get no reply and it was too dark to try and trail him. I did not know that there was any one on the creek but myself.

I did not go to bed that night, thinking where could Fitz be. The next morning as soon as light began to dawn I fixed up a lunch, as Fitz never took any when he went shooting, and started on his trail up the mountain, and I could trail him to within one bench of the top and no farther, as the mountains were bare above and it was snowing and blowing a gale. One could not keep their feet all of the time, yet I kept on until part way up and to the right to a draw and there I discovered that there had been a snow slide of recent date and crawled around the head of it, but could find no tracks and as the storm was increasing I was compelled to turn back down the mountains. Then I started down the creek to get help to look for Fitz.

I found two men who had come up to 21 above and a man there who was going down into Big Manook where some men were at work took the news that Fitz was lost. The two men, a Mr. N. Nelson and his partner came up the next morning at daylight and we started up the mountains again, but as it was storming so bad that a man could not live on the mountain or stand upon his feet, we were compelled to turn back again. I sent word to town that Fitz was lost in the mountains, and Mr. J. Duncan, of the A. E. Co., and a Mr. Weber, of the same company, came out with a dog team prepared to stay until we found him.

Thursday morning, the 8th, it came out very pleasant and seven of us started out early and went up the mountain where I found the last trail of him and began to search. The wind had blown the snow off of the old snow so that we found tracks leading up to the side but could find nothing more there but upon the other side of the slide we found where he had come past the slide. After a little we found tracks leading back to where the snow had slid and an empty shell that he had thrown away, and could find no place where he had come off of the slide. Then we began to go over the slide, Duncan and Weber down the outside, Weber in the lead and Duncan close behind.

As Weber stepped in the snow up to his knee Duncan came along and poked the snow out of the hole with his hand and found the muzzle of his shotgun staring him in the face. Then Duncan called, "Boys, here is his gun, and the poor boy must be here somewhere."

Appendix

I beg to call to your attention to the "Arctic Mining, Trading and Transportation Company," chartered by the State of Illinois with a capital of $20,000 apportioned in 200 shares with par value of $100 each.

The stock of this concern has been entirely subscribed by four individuals, a limited amount being re-assigned in trust to the Treasurer for sale at $25 per share, fully paid and non-assessable.

It will be the object of the Officers and Directors of the Company to employ in a conservative and economical manner, every sensible means for the discovery of precious ores in Alaska and also to seek opportunities for investment in any other legitimate lines— in which a country so rich in natural resources must surely abound—such as merchandising, trading in furs, etc., and establishing transportation lines. To accomplish these objects it is not at first necessary to have millions of capital, and sell stock like the sands of the sea. If the enterprise proves successful, the fewer interested, the better, and it is an easy matter to secure additional capital when our merit is established.

Our chief aim for the present will be to afford the opportunity to conservative business men and women for investing small sums in [properly] exploring the resources of Alaska, believing that in "Union there is strength," and that two hundred people contributing $25 each to a common fund may accomplish for all what to one alone would be an impossibility.

Our mining engineer, Mr. R. Hunter Fitzhugh, sails from Seattle, September the [10th] on the Steamer "Portland" direct for the Yukon River, Alaska. He will be one of the best equipped men who ever prospected in that region.

If you care to invest in one or more shares of the stock, we shall be pleased to hear from you at once, and to furnish you further particulars if desired. The time for action, however, is brief, and the number of shares offered for sale limited.

Yours very truly,

Hunter Fitzhugh [signature]

N. B. No more that 10 shares will be sold to any single purchaser, his or her immediate family.

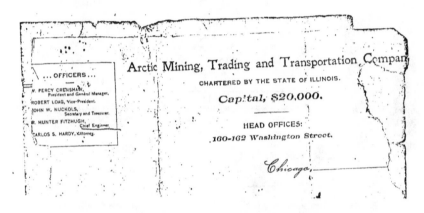

Copy of the original letterhead on which the letter which follows appeared. This letter also appeared as a newspaper advertisement on May 8, 1897.

THE FITZHUGH FAMILY TREE

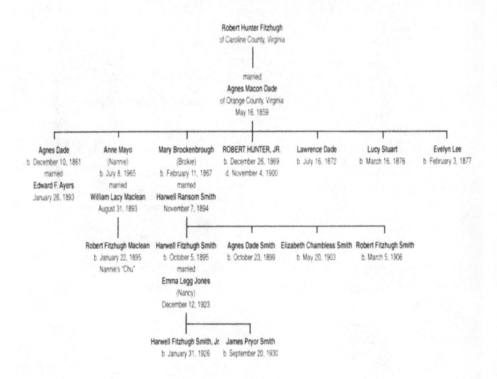

Robert Hunter Fitzhugh
of Caroline County, Virginia

married
Agnes Macon Dade
of Orange County, Virginia
May 16, 1859

Agnes Dade	Anne Mayo	Mary Brockenbrough	ROBERT HUNTER, JR.	Lawrence Dade	Lucy Stuart	Evelyn Lee
b. December 10, 1861	(Nannie)	(Brokie)	b. December 26, 1869	b. July 16, 1872	b. March 16, 1876	b. February 3, 1877
married	b. July 8, 1965	b. February 11, 1867	d. November 4, 1900			
Edward F. Ayers	married	married				
January 26, 1893	William Lacy Maclean	Harwell Ransom Smith				
	August 31, 1893	November 7, 1894				

Robert Fitzhugh Maclean
b. January 22, 1895
Nannie's "Chu"

Harwell Fitzhugh Smith
b. October 5, 1895
married
Emma Legg Jones
(Nancy)
December 12, 1923

Agnes Dade Smith
b. October 23, 1899

Elizabeth Chambless Smith
b. May 20, 1903

Robert Fitzhugh Smith
b. March 5, 1906

Harwell Fitzhugh Smith, Jr.
b. January 31, 1926

James Pryor Smith
b. September 20, 1930

(From left) Mary Brockenbrough Fitzhugh (Mrs. Harwell R. Smith, Hunter's sister), Elizabeth Chambless Smith (Dickerson), Robert Fitzhugh Smith, Agnes Macon Dade Fitzhugh (Hunter's mother), Harwell Fitzhugh Smith, Sr.

Hunter my "chum brother" was always one of the dearest most interesting parts of my life. From our earliest child-

Three of Hunter's sisters (from left) Anne ("Nannie"), Agnes Dade ("Daisy"), and Mary ("Brokie")

hood we were partners and confidants. Many a long expedition waling over

Above: Reproduction of the Fitzhugh family Bible page recording Hunter's death. Opposite page: A page written by Hunter's sister Mary Brockenbrough Fitzhugh Smith (Brokie). The text is transcribed here:

hill and field did we go together. Fall after fall we wandered over the South Frankfort hills gathering walnuts. Later summer after summer we went black berrying in Carrolton always happy to be together though hard at work.

Alter he left home he twice sent me money for fine trips and it was on

Hunter, my "chum brother," was always one of the dearest most interesting parts of my life. From our earliest childhood we were partners and confidants.

Many a long expedition walking over hill and field did we go together. Fall after fall we wandered over the South Frankfort hills gathering walnuts. Later summer after summer we went black berrying "Carrollton" always happy to be together though hard at work.

After he left home he three sent me money for fine trips and it was for one of these, that I met Harwell. After he went to the Klon- dyke, we corresponded regularly and confidentially up to four days before his death. He and I knew so many people and things in common, remembered the same things and had so many experiences together that his loss leaves a great vacancy in my mind as a reference and as the one who understands.

one of these that I met Harwell.

    After he went to the Klondyke [sic] we corresponded regularly and confidentially up to four days before his death. H and I knew so many people and things in common, remembered the same things had so many experiences together that he leaves a great vacancy in my mind and a refer- ence and one who understands.

Photo Credits

41   73-50-10N, Paul Cyr Collection, Alaska and Polar Regions Archives, Rasmuson, Library, University of Alaska, Fairbanks

51   Courtesy of Alaska State Library/James Wickersham Collection/PCA 277-1-9

58   61-1022-66N, Historical Photo Collection, Alaska and Polar Regions Archives, Rasmuson Library, University of Alaska, Fairbanks

60   Courtesy of Alaska State Library/James Wickersham Collection/PCA 277-9-26

67   Fitzhugh family

77   Courtesy of Alaska State Library/Winter & Pond Collection/PCA 87-1106

81   Photograph by Pillsbury & Cleveland/"Rampart City on the Yukon, 1899"/Courtesy of Alaska State Library/Panoramic Views of Alaska Collection/PCA 63-11B

93   73-50-7N, Paul Cyr Collection, Alaska and Polar Regions Archives, Rasmuson Library, University of Alaska, Fairbanks

94   64-92-430, Selid-Bassoc Photo Collection, Alaska and Polar Regions Archives, Rasmuson Library, University of Alaska, Fairbanks

95   83-209-65N, Historical Photo Collection, Alaska and Polar Regions Archives, Rasmuson Library, University of Alaska, Fairbanks

98   64-92-719, Selid-Bassoc Photo Collection, Alaska and Polar Regions Archives, Rasmuson Library, University of Alaska, Fairbanks

101   Courtesy of Alaska State Library/Case & Draper Collection/PCA 39-843

104   61-1022-49, Historical Photo Collection, Alaska and Polar Regions Archives, Rasmuson Library, University of Alaska, Fairbanks

105   83-149-1895N, Stephen R. Capps Collection, Alaska and Polar Regions Archives, Rasmuson Library, University of Alaska, Fairbanks

108   67-17-20N, H. Levy Collection, Alaska and Polar Regions Archives, Rasmuson Library, University of Alaska, Fairbanks

109   "On the Yukon, Rampart"/Courtesy of Alaska State Library/Clarence L. Andrews Collection/PCA 45-277

117–
121   Fitzhugh family

CPSIA information can be obtained
at www.ICGtesting.com
Printed in the USA
JSHW041310100521
14568JS00001B/101